Henry Clay
and the
Art of
American Politics

Library of Congress Catalog Card No. 57-5825

ISBN 0-316-20412-9

Z Y X W

ALP

Published simultaneously in Canada
by Little, Brown & Company (Canada) Limited

Printed in the United States of America

Clement Eaton

Henry Clay
and the
Art of
American Politics

Edited by Oscar Handlin

Little, Brown and Company • *Boston* • *Toronto*

*To those politicians, living and dead,
who like my father have endeavored
to make politics an honorable and
courageous profession
in the United States*

Editor's Preface

IN THE SECOND DECADE of the nineteenth century political power in America shifted into the hands of a new generation. The young men of the period that then began had not themselves participated in the process of Constitution-making and they accepted the general outline of government as the founders of the Republic had left it. Until the Civil War there would be few significant efforts to tamper with the Constitution.

The new era's political innovations were of another order. The nation's rapid expansion presented Americans with perplexing issues as its statesmen grappled with the problems of foreign affairs, tariff, finance, and internal improvements. The very size and diversity of the country generated contending and often contradictory interests. It was the function of democratic politics in this period to resolve those conflicts through compromise.

The instrument of compromise was the political party, a device the founders of the Republic had scarcely envisioned. The essence of the party was the coalition cemented together in it of various interests and sections. Its operations therefore centered in the Congress and particularly in the Senate, where there gradually evolved the two parties that were to organize American political life in the two decades after 1830.

By his situation as the representative of Kentucky, a border state, and by his personal qualities, Henry Clay found himself involved in all these trends. His successes and his failures dramatically illustrated the developing qualities of politics in a democracy. Clement Eaton's illuminating account reveals the man in his relationship to these significant trends.

OSCAR HANDLIN

Contents

Henry Clay
and the
Art of
American Politics

I

The Promised Land

In the autumn of 1797 a slim and gangling youth of twenty rode through the Cumberland Gap to Kentucky. Henry Clay, with a license just issued by the Virginia courts to practice law, was entering the Promised Land of the West to begin a great career in American politics. Through the years that lay ahead he was to serve his country as Speaker of the House of Representatives, leader of the War Hawks in 1812, peace commissioner at Ghent, Secretary of State, candidate of the national Republican and Whig parties for President, and senator from Kentucky, who more than any other statesman of his era contributed to preserving the Union. In the estimation of many of his contemporaries and of later students as well, he became the epitome of the American politician.

At this time, upon his entrance into Kentucky, his rustic appearance and homespun suit gave little indication of his remarkable qualities. His tall, loosely constructed figure was propelled by a peculiar gait, "stately but swinging." So mobile and sensitive was his face that numerous painters and sculptors failed to achieve a faithful likeness. His eyes were blue, his complexion fair, and he himself confessed that his chin was "not remarkable." His whimsical mouth was so wide that he could scarcely whistle or practice the manly art of spitting tobacco juice with reasonable accuracy. In his young manhood his blond hair seemed almost white, but in later life became dark brown in color.

When young Clay crossed the mountains, he entered a "Promised Land." In the year before, Moses Austin had traveled along the same Wilderness Road, passing a procession of pioneers climbing through the historic gap on their way to settle on land "rich as cream." Many were ragged and without shoes or stockings, but they were spurred on by the hope of finding a better life beyond the Cumberland Mountains. Despite the fact that they had no money with which to pay for Western land, they had a naïve faith that they could obtain it somehow, perhaps by "squatting" upon it. "Can anything be more Absurd than the Conduct of man," Austin asked. "Here is hundreds Traveling hundreds of Miles they know not for what Nor Whither, except its to Kentuckey, passing land almost as good and easy obtain . . . but it will not do, its not Kentuckey its not the Promisd land its not the goodly inheratence the Land of Milk and Honey, and when arrivd at this Heaven in Idea what do they find? a goodly land I will allow but to them forbiden Land."

Young Henry Clay too was penniless, but Kentucky proved for him a land of exciting opportunity. Years later, he wrote, "I am in one respect better off than Moses. He died in sight of and without reaching the Promised Land. I occupy so good a farm as any he would have found had he reached it, and Ashland [his plantation near Lexington] has been acquired not by hereditary descent but by my own labor." The fluid society of the new West permitted a young man who had nothing but energy and ability to attain the status of an English country gentleman and to aspire to become President of the United States.

Like most of the settlers of Kentucky, Clay bore no credentials of family influence or prominent connections. He had been born on a farm in Virginia on April 12, 1777. His father was a Baptist preacher in a region where the aristocrats were Church of England adherents. Of his ancestors he knew little except that they had come from England in the seventeenth century. To an inquiry about his genealogy, he replied many years later that he had always been too busy to investigate the lineage of his ancestors and now since he had become old, he said, "I shall so soon meet them in another, and I hope better state that I have thought it hardly necessary to institute any inquiry." To a biographer who wished to display a coat of arms on the cover of his biography, Clay wrote that he had none and in any case preferred an emblem associated with his political career, "a loom, shuttle, anvil, plow or any other article connected with manufactures, agriculture, or commerce."

After the democratic movement of the 1830's made it good politics to appeal to the common man, campaign orators and Clay himself exaggerated his humble origin. Actually, he was born in a story-and-a-half frame house superior to the homes of the average Virginia farmers. In 1840 he visited his birthplace, near Hanover Court House, fifteen miles north of Richmond. After an absence of forty-eight years he found the old dwelling still standing but much altered from its appearance in his boyhood. The church where he attended school for two years had also decayed. The unmarked graves of his father and grandparents were overgrown with wheat; the hickory tree which had produced the finest nuts that he had ever tasted was prostrate. But the row of May cherry trees that he knew in childhood was still in part standing.

Clay often thought back to the poverty and hard work of his boyhood. When a plow manufacturer of Louisville in 1842 presented him with a Kentucky plow, he replied that among his earliest recollections was a memory of following the plow. One of the appealing legends that campaign orators and biographers created was that of the youthful Clay riding to mill, with a sack of wheat or corn on his pony's back, "the mill-boy of the Slashes" (the "Slashes" being the name given to Clay's rather poor neighborhood).

Clay's family, however, belonged actually to a much more prosperous class of society than the poor-boy legend indicated. His father, curiously called "Sir John," died when Henry was four years old. The widow, Elizabeth, quickly remarried and had a large family — seven children by her new husband, Captain Stephen Watkins, to add to her first family of nine. In 1782 she owned eighteen slaves and four hundred and sixty-four acres of land, taxed at twice the value of the average in the county. Henry's father left a farm, Euphraium, in Henrico County, which the widow and her second husband illegally sold when they removed to Kentucky. John Clay, according to his distinguished son, was "much embarrassed" financially when he died, but he left Henry and his two surviving brothers two slaves each. In 1823 they recovered ownership of their father's farm by legal action.

Henry's education was badly neglected. Three years in the school of Peter Deacon, an intemperate Englishman, and some instruction from his parents constituted the whole of his early education. Throughout his later life he felt keenly the lack of a sound classical training. He lamented this deficiency in a letter to his son Henry, confessing that he had never studied half enough. He especially regretted that he had not studied Latin and Greek, a knowledge of which in his time was the hallmark of the educated man. This lack of formal schooling may have produced a superficiality of reasoning that "remained one of his weak points through life."

In 1792, when he was fifteen years old, his mother and stepfather emigrated to Versailles, Kentucky, in the Bluegrass country, where they kept a tavern. They left him behind "without guardian or money." But his stepfather secured for him a place as a deputy clerk in the High Court of Chancery. Here he attracted the attention of George Wythe, a signer of the Declaration of Independence, the first professor of law in America, and then Chancellor of Virginia. Disabled by a crippled hand, Wythe selected the young Clay, who had a neat and legible handwriting, to be his secretary. Thus the impressionable youth came under the influence of one of the great men of Virginia, a fine classical scholar, and a man of liberal opinions, in favor of the gradual emancipation of the slaves. Highly respected for his stern Republican virtue, he was a bachelor who had a mulatto son whom he carefully educated in his household.

Wythe discovered that his young amanuensis had a bright mind and a spirit eager to learn. He directed the reading of his protégé to translations of the classics, particularly to Homer and Plutarch, and to law books. After getting a start in the study of law under Wythe's direction Clay entered the law office of Robert Brooke, a former governor of the state, where he studied in preparation for the bar examination.

In November, 1797, after he had been granted a license to practice law in Virginia, he left his native state to make a career for himself in Kentucky. He stopped for a few months at the home of his parents in Versailles and then settled in Lexington. Into this thriving little community in the Bluegrass young Clay's amiable and largely extroverted personality fitted easily. The society of Lexington was too young and too Western to have become exclusive or highly stratified. Furthermore, the newcomer was not handicapped by excessive timidity, for bold confidence was ever characteristic of his nature.

Kentucky in Clay's young manhood was largely an extension into the Western country of the Piedmont and the Valley society of Virginia. François André Michaux, the French botanist, described the inhabitants as nearly all natives of Virginia who had preserved the manners of the mother state. Like the Virginians, they exhibited a passion for gambling, drinking spirituous liquors to excess, and owning fine horses — not draft horses, however. "Horses and law-suits," he reported, "comprise the usual topic of their conversation." Similar to the custom of the inhabitants of rural and isolated communities in America generally, Kentuckians asked the passing traveler a thousand questions. At the same time they were very hospitable, offering the stranger a glass of whiskey or inviting him to their homes.

The French traveler found that with the exception of the upper class, the Kentuckians were devoted to evangelical religion, although not bigoted as to denominationalism. He noted their public spirit, especially in trying to introduce new products into the state. He found provisions very cheap, skilled labor high, and specie so scarce that the inhabitants cut the silver dollar into four, eight, and sixteen parts while merchants depended on barter for trade. Finally, he was impressed with their pride and boastfulness in regard to their state. "The inhabitants of Kentucky," he observed, "eagerly recommend to strangers the country they inhabit as the best part of the United States, as that where the soil is most fertile, the climate most salubrious, and where all the inhabitants were brought through the love of liberty and independence."

Other travelers noted that this society had its faults, in which young Henry Clay shared. The people were "frank, affable, polite, and hospitable," yet quick in temper and sudden in resentment; they "drink a great deal, swear a great deal, and gamble a great deal." Kind to strangers, particularly to stranded travelers who were sick and without money, they carried and used savage dirks; their cock fighting, gander pulling, dueling, spitting tobacco juice, barbecues, hasty eating in taverns, flogging Negro slaves, and general indolence reflected the rural character of the state or the crudity of the West.

Lexington, where Clay made his home, was a delightful place. The scenery about the town was not dramatic but pleasant and reposeful, with undulating green hills, parks shaded at intervals by honey locust and oak trees, and pools of water, often artificially made for watering the flocks and herds that grazed upon the lush bluegrass. In May, when the delicate blue flowers of the grass were in full bloom, a field of Kentucky grass gave an illusion of a lavender-colored carpet spread on the ground. While districts near the Ohio River raised tobacco, the great money crop of the region was hemp, which only slightly exhausted the fertile limestone soil.

The town itself at the end of the eighteenth century contained some two thousand white and black people. It would double in size in the next ten years. The center of trade for Kentucky, it boasted also of its growing and diversified industries. Breweries, distilleries, nail factories, hat factories, powder mills, ropewalks, and textile mills were among the enterprises that developed in the decade after Clay arrived. Among the artisans were silversmiths who fashioned julep cups, bowls, pitchers, tableware, and jewelry, often from "coin silver."

Transportation was the vital life stream in the rapid growth of these Western towns. The main highway of

Lexington led to the Ohio River at Limestone (later called Maysville). This was the route used by John Bradford to transport the first printing press brought into Kentucky, on which the *Gazette* was published in 1787; and it was the route of the merchants in bringing their stock of goods from Philadelphia or Baltimore. The Maysville Road wound along steep curves through its hilly section and was often muddy and difficult to travel. Clay reported as late as 1829 that he and his family were forced to spend nearly four days traveling between Maysville and Lexington, a distance of sixty-four miles. No wonder that he was outraged when Jackson vetoed the Maysville Turnpike bill! On several occasions, notably in the fall of 1850, when he was a frail old man, his coach was overturned as he journeyed along Zane's Trace and the National Road to Washington. The Ohio River route was also used by Clay and his family, especially in returning from the East or going to New Orleans, but it was closed at times to navigation by ice or low water. In a speech at Pittsburgh made late in his life he reminisced that he had often purchased "one of those arks, or Kentucky flatboats as they were called, divided and fitted it into separate compartments of Stable, Kitchen, and Parlour, and in that way floated my family and myself down the current of the beautiful river." Clay sent his mules and horses to the Southern market along the Wilderness Road, which crossed the mountains through Cumberland Gap.

Lexington was an inland town, fifteen miles from the Kentucky River. Its remoteness from the Atlantic seaboard served virtually as a protective tariff for the infant industries of the town, encouraging a diversified manufacturing economy. After the introduction of the steamboat on the Mississippi and Ohio rivers, however, Lexington could no longer compete with the Ohio River towns. The voyage of the *Enterprise,* the first steamboat to make the upriver trip from New Orleans to Louisville, in 1815 marked the beginning of Lexington's downfall as the emporium of the West. Quickly thereafter Louisville and Cincinnati absorbed much of Lexington's trade and surpassed the Bluegrass capital in population and wealth.

Yet Lexington retained its supremacy as the intellectual and social center of Kentucky, "the Athens of the West." Here was located Transylvania University, the oldest university west of the Appalachian Mountains. The town supported a public library, a museum, and an athenaeum, where subscribers could read newspapers from all over the United States as well as the principal English periodicals. The citizens patronized the local artist, Matthew Jouett, who painted portraits of the aristocrats and notables of the Bluegrass, including an early portrait of Clay. It had French dancing teachers, academies, two newspapers, and a good literary magazine, the *Western Review.*

But the most important element of culture was a nucleus of aristocratic people in the town and on neighboring plantations, chiefly Virginians, such as the planter David Meade, educated at Harrow, who lived in a charming home, Chaumière des Prairies, a few miles from Lexington. In the town the professional people, lawyers, doctors, artists, and professors, such as the naturalist Constantine Rafinesque or the brilliant liberal president of Transylvania University, Horace Holley, gave a tone of refinement and good breeding to Bluegrass society.

When Clay began his career as a lawyer in Lexington, he did not have, he reminisced, "the means of paying" his "weekly board." He was delighted when he received his first fee of fifteen shillings. Although the bar of Lexington was quite distinguished by its able lawyers, such as John Breckinridge, George Nicholas, and James Brown, young

Clay was remarkably successful from the outset. By 1805 he had prospered to such an extent that James Brown, his brother-in-law, who had removed to New Orleans, wrote to him that he had heard from Kentuckians visiting New Orleans that Clay stood at the head of his profession and was rapidly growing rich. "Indeed," he commented, "some accounts assure us that you are acquiring money 'as fast as you can count it.' "

Since Lexington was the metropolis of Kentucky at this time, there was abundant opportunity for Clay to make money not only in legal practice but in investing his profits in land speculations and manufacturing. In this new country, where money was scarce, some of his clients paid their legal fees in horses and land. Clay acquired town lots, bought the Kentucky Hotel in Lexington, and speculated in land in Missouri and Ohio. Most of the legal business of Kentucky was concerned with land, Negro slaves, and the collection of debts for Eastern merchants. Clay apparently was the attorney for a Baltimore merchant, William Taylor, to whom in 1803 he sent a large sum of money by horseback, $2000 of specie per horse (he wrote to his client that he had tried in vain to procure bank bills with which to dispatch the money).

On April 11, 1799, he married Lucretia Hart in the Hart home on Mill Street in Lexington. Clay's marriage into this family brought him into the circle of the developing Bluegrass aristocracy. Colonel Thomas Hart, Lucretia's father, was one of the early settlers of Kentucky and was prominent in the group of merchants, hemp manufacturers, and planters that dominated the life of the town. As manager of Colonel Hart's legal business, the young lawyer profited both economically and politically from family connections, which offered a powerful political advantage in the Old South.

Clay's personality must have played a large part in his

success as a lawyer. Possessing a fluent tongue, an actor's ability, and a keen knowledge of the psychology of frontier juries, he did not need much knowledge of the law to win criminal cases. In the courtroom he was quick to take advantage of technical points of law and to use humor and sarcasm to discredit a hostile witness or opposing counsel. An opportunist in legal practice who studied the faces of the jury, he quickly adapted his argument to their prejudices and changing moods. One of his tricks was to crouch low and then rise to his full height as he drove home an argument. George D. Prentice, a Connecticut Yankee who came to Lexington in 1830 to write the first biography of Clay, states that despite the great number of criminal cases which Clay defended, "not one of his clients was ever sentenced to death." Actually in 1799 Clay lost what was probably his first capital case, that of Henry Field, a planter of Woodford County, who, despite Clay's eloquent plea, was convicted of killing his wife. The evidence for the conviction was circumstantial, and several months after he was hanged, one of his female slaves confessed to the murder. Thus Clay appears to have "flunked" his first major test at the bar. Afterwards, however, this eloquent and plausible lawyer was responsible for the acquittal of many a criminal who should have been punished.

Politics, not the profession of law, became Clay's great obsession, however. His first adventure in politics was an attack on the economic interests and conservative point of view of the ruling class. In 1798-1799 a campaign to call a constitutional convention in order to democratize the government and to make it possible for the state gradually to emancipate its slaves aroused great excitement in Kentucky. In championing the emancipation cause Clay spoke boldly against aristocratic control of the government. After the passage of the Alien and Sedition Acts he won favor from all classes by denouncing these oppressive laws in an eloquent speech before a large crowd assembled in a field near Lexington. The audience was so enthusiastic that they carried him in triumph from the field. In the presidential election of 1800 he was an ardent supporter of Thomas Jefferson and the principles of the Republican party.

Three years later he was elected to the legislature as a representative of Fayette County. While he was stump-speaking during the campaign, a frontiersman in his audience challenged him to show his fitness for political office by shooting at a target. Clay promptly accepted the challenge, borrowed a rifle, and hit the target nearly in the center. Thus he won the vote of the backwoodsman and the applause of the crowd. In describing the episode, so Daniel Mallory his biographer in 1843 reported, Clay said, "I had never before fired a rifle, and have not since."

In the legislature his efforts were devoted mainly to trying to move the state capital from Frankfort to Lexington and to defending the Kentucky Insurance Company. This company had been incorporated by the legislature in 1802 for the declared object of insuring cargoes on the Ohio and Mississippi rivers and their tributaries. The charter, however, which conferred a monopoly upon the company for fifteen years, permitted it to engage in the banking business by issuing notes to an unlimited amount. In 1804 Felix Grundy, an ambitious lawyer and politician of Clay's age, began a movement in the legislature to repeal the monopolistic charter of the company. The repeal was very popular with the common people but opposed by the conservative business interests of Lexington. Young Clay fought zealously in the legislature to protect the privileges of the company and ultimately saved its monopolistic charter by an adroit political maneuver.

While he was in the legislature he participated in a spectacular legal case, the trial of Aaron Burr at Frank fort. On November 5, 1806, the federal district attorney, Joseph Hamilton Daveiss, an ardent admirer of Alexander Hamilton, whom Burr had killed in a duel, indicted the adventurer for promoting a filibuster expedition against the Spanish territory beyond the Mississippi. Burr asked Clay and Colonel John Allen to serve as counsel. Believing the accused to be innocent and the charge against him to have been motivated by Federalist malice, Clay undertook his defense. The grand jury at Frankfort after hearing the evidence acquitted the distinguished defendant. When Burr sent "a considerable fee" to his counsel they generously declined to accept it. Two weeks after the acquittal Daveiss renewed legal action against the former Republican leader. Again Burr appealed to Clay to serve as his counsel. Since the young Kentuckian had recently been elected to the Senate to fill an unexpired term, he requested his client to give him written assurance that he was engaged in no treasonable or illegal undertaking. Burr wrote the desired letter, and Clay and Allen accordingly again represented him. A second time the jury acquitted Burr and when its verdict was announced, a shouting and rejoicing arose among the audience such as Clay said that he had never before witnessed in Kentucky.

Shortly thereafter, Clay journeyed northward on his way to take his seat in the Senate. At Chillicothe, Ohio, he vigorously defended Burr from the charge of treason. But when he arrived in Washington he was shown evidence by President Jefferson that convinced him of Burr's guilt. Some years later he accidentally met Burr in New York, but when the intriguer offered his hand, Clay refused it. Despite Clay's innocence of any complicity in treasonable designs, he was accused of being a "Burrite," and later in his political career he had to refute the charge.

Clay was only twenty-nine years old when he took his seat in the Senate and was thus illegally seated. Although his term of office lasted only a few months, it gave him a taste of Washington official life. Regarding it as primarily a tour of pleasure, according to the New Hampshire Senator Plumer, he gambled much, read little, and was "out almost every night," being very popular with the ladies.

At this carefree stage of his life, he frequently gambled for high stakes. He told Plumer that on one evening he had won fifteen hundred dollars at cards and on the next evening lost six hundred. His optimism and superb confidence in himself were carried into his amusements, particularly his reckless reliance on luck in playing poker and brag. In 1812 he confessed to his friend Caesar Rodney, "You know, Rodney, that I have always paid peculiar homage to the fickle goddess." Senator George Poindexter of Mississippi later told of playing brag with Clay when the latter, "stung to madness by his losses," wagered the hotel which he owned.

Upon his return from Washington in 1807 Clay was re-elected to the lower house of the state legislature. Here he ardently championed the leading measures of Jefferson's administration. The recent *Chesapeake–Leopard* affair had aroused public feeling against Great Britain so much that a bill was introduced forbidding the citations of any British legal decision in the courts of Kentucky. Its enactment would have destroyed the common law in the state. Although Clay shared the Anglophobia of other Kentuckians, he stepped down from the Speaker's chair to argue against the passage of this disastrous measure. The legislature finally adopted a compromise, proposed by him, which excluded from citation in the courts of the state only those British decisions rendered after July 4, 1776.

In supporting Republican measures the young legislator frequently encountered in debate the leading Federalist of Kentucky, Humphrey Marshall, a tall, dark, aristocratic lawyer who possessed a sarcastic tongue and a great disdain for the rabble. He had become hostile to Clay as a result of the Burr affair, and now he clashed with him on the floor of the house of representatives over national politics. On January 3, 1809, Clay introduced a resolution that the members of the legislature show their patriotism by wearing homespun suits instead of British broadcloth. Marshall was one of two legislators who voted against the resolution. Shortly thereafter he appeared in the legislature flaunting a fine English broadcloth suit while Clay wore homespun. During the course of debate Marshall accused Clay of playing the demagogue. This charge infuriated the young speaker, who rushed at Marshall to administer a physical beating. But a huge German representative, General Christopher Riffe, held the antagonists apart, saying, "Come poys, no fighting here. I vips you both."

Clay then challenged Marshall to a duel, which took place on January 9 at Shippingport, Indiana, a village opposite Louisville. Clay's letter describing this his first duel has the ring of youthful pride and elation: "I have this moment returned from the field of battle. We had three shots. On the first I grazed him just above the navel — he missed me. On the second my damned pistol snapped and he missed me. On the third I rec'd a flesh wound in the thigh, and owing to my receiving the fire first etc., I missed him."

Although Henry Clay was a debonair young man, eager for fun, reckless and hedonistic, the cavalier myth of Clay has exaggerated these "Prince Hal" or "Gallant Hal" characteristics. Actually he was also very ambitious and displayed a tremendous capacity for hard work. In his

youth at Richmond he had been a member of a debat
ing society and in Lexington he joined a similar club
to improve himself in public speaking. He always enjoyed
a glass of wine and bought imported Madeira and sherry
by the cask (one receipted bill for imported wine in his
papers, dated September 18, 1838, amounted to $302.04).
The earliest recollection of Clay by J. O. Harrison, his
friend and executor, was seeing him during a court trial
pour out a glass of claret and "treat the opposing counsel
to it."

During these buoyant years Clay's life was characterized by an uninhibited quality which gradually disappeared as he grew older and more circumspect. At this
time, for example, his wit was more suited to the Western
country store than to the parlors of *grandes dames*. To
Colonel George Thompson, near Harrodsburg, Kentucky,
he wrote in such a vein of humor on March 14, 1810, from
the Senate Chamber: "Bonaparte has repudiated the Empress. I suspect he is afraid of being denominated a fum-
bler, and wishes to operate on a subject more prolific
than the Empress. His brother's wife Miss Patterson alias
the Dutchess has been figuring away here some time, with
her little son. I would recommend her to imitate her
brother-in-law's example and take to herself a good strong
back Democrat. She looks as if she wanted very much the
services of such a character." As to Kentucky, he boasted,
"We have the finest country in the world, and he who has
seen it and *doubts* it ought to receive the punishment
denounced agt. unbelievers."

This enthusiastic young Kentuckian set out to win a
career for himself in politics in democratic America. He
was highly gifted to realize his ambitions. He was flexible
— his severe critics called him an opportunist — so that he
could adapt himself to the rapidly changing political
scene of the United States. His character at the same time

was much above the standard of the ordinary politician, though based as it was on a romantic sense of honor rather than on Christian precepts. Perhaps because he was poorly educated, he tended to scorn theory and, like his Western neighbors, to settle problems on a pragmatic and immediate basis. America in his time loved an orator and Clay became a master of eloquent speech and of polemics. He was an optimist, a booster, having a temperament exactly suited to the mood of the West and a growing country. Bold and decisive, he was a natural leader who had nothing of the Hamlet psychology in his make-up; he did not weigh the pros and cons of a situation or agonize or hesitate over decisions. His impulsive and ardent nature led him to take people into his confidence and to speak out on public questions. Attracted by these qualities, the citizens of his district elected him again and again to be their representative in Congress, where he was to stand forth as the ardent spokesman of the West.

I I

Spokesman of the West

THE KENTUCKY LEGISLATURE in January, 1810,
chose Clay to fill out another unexpired term in the
Senate. During the next five years he was to become the
strongest and the most appealing leader in Congress. He
was also to represent his country as a peace commissioner
at Ghent. He was to have the satisfaction that few men
enjoy of devoting himself to a patriotic cause and at the
same time of advancing his personal interests and ambitions. These were the years of seed time, when his nationalistic ideas began to germinate.

In 1811 when Clay traveled to Congress he carried in
his coach a bottle of Kentucky wine to present to President Madison. A note accompanying the bottle character-
istically expressed the pride of a Western man in the
products of his region. Throughout his long political career Henry Clay regarded himself as a Westerner. Although Virginian by birth and rearing, he absorbed the
vibrant, go-ahead, boastful spirit of his adopted environ-
ment, the New West. Democratic and natural in manners,
moreover, he retained to the end of his life some of the
salient qualities associated with the rise of the Western

country — optimism, self-confidence, impatience with theory, and strong national feeling.

The key to his career in national politics was his endeavor to form an alliance between the young, relatively undeveloped West and the industrial North. He became as a result a kind of Western doughface. Many years later he wrote to Horace Greeley concerning some resolutions and a speech he had made in Lexington against the Mexican War, "Will they [the public] not represent me as a Western man (I protest against being considered a Southern man) with Northern principles." His colorful personality and his attention to Western interests earned him such sobriquets as "Gallant Harry of the West," "the Cock of Kentucky," "the Western Hotspur," "the Judas of the West," "the Western Candidate," and "the Western Star."

It was an essential requirement of American politics in Clay's period that a Congressman should represent the local feeling and interests of his region. Clay, in common with most of his colleagues in Congress, believed that he should obey the instructions of his constituents as to how he should vote on bills and resolutions. De Tocqueville, who traveled in the United States in 1831-1832, observed that it was a peculiar characteristic of American politics that a member in Congress spoke frequently and often in elevated language in Congress for the benefit of "the folks back home." Thus the politician who was active and eloquent in Congress administered to state pride and let the nation know of the greatness of his state.

Therefore, when Clay took his seat as senator in the winter of 1810, he realized that he had an obligation to participate actively in the business of the Senate. Lexington had become an ambitious little town with an expanding group of infant industries, and the hemp interests of the Bluegrass needed tariff protection. Clay therefore advocated a protective tariff. Also, the West, with its eye on the outlet of the Mississippi River, was in favor of seizing West Florida from Spain, and accordingly Clay supported such a policy.

Again, the West opposed the recharter of the First Bank of the United States. Clay obeyed instructions of the legislature and voted against the recharter bill. He spoke vigorously against the maintenance of a national bank in which the federal government was only a minority partner. He referred to the danger that British stockholders who owned two thirds of the stock might influence American affairs. Thus he catered to the rampant Anglophobia of the West. Contrary to his later constitutional principles, he argued for a strict interpretation of the federal Constitution. Later in his career Clay came to feel that his vote against the bank in 1811 was a mistake — and he frankly confessed that he had erred.

In the spring of 1811, in a speech well attuned to Western interests and prejudices, Clay threw his support behind the movement to force a declaration of war against Great Britain. Incensed by the belief that the British in Canada were inciting and giving aid to the Indians in attacking the American frontier, he declared that war with Great Britain could extinguish "the torch that lights up savage warfare." In a great flourish of oratory and Western bravado he declared that the militia of Kentucky alone could take Montreal and Upper Canada.

In the summer of that year he was elected a representative to the lower house of Congress. He preferred, he said, the excitement and activity of the House of Representatives to "the solemn stillness" of the Senate. At his first appearance in the House of Representatives he was chosen Speaker. "Harry of the West" became one of the best and most powerful Speakers that the House of Representatives has ever had. When he assumed the office in

1811 the Speaker was little more than a presiding officer. But Clay made the position one of party leadership and by his precedents immeasurably strengthened the office. Six times he was elected Speaker and never was his election seriously contested.

He was the boldest and most decisive, perhaps, of the long line of Speakers of the House of Representatives. He used his power to push his favorite measures through Congress. Not content merely to listen, he would often speak on important issues when they were debated in the committee of the whole. He presided with dignity and grace and tolerated no disrespect of himself or the House. Relatively unlearned in parliamentary procedure, he made his decisions on the basis of common sense and what was expedient and practical. Out of his experience he gave to Robert C. Winthrop, who became Speaker in 1847, the shrewd advice: "Decide, decide promptly, and never give your reasons for the decision. The House will sustain your decisions, but there will always be men to cavil and quarrel about your reasons." Despite a tendency to be imperious, he treated the members with unfailing tact and courtesy and therefore was very popular.

Before Clay became Speaker, John Randolph of Roanoke had ridden rough-shod over the presiding officer of the House and had ignored the rules of that body. One of America's great eccentrics, Randolph had such a caustic tongue and such a devilishly clever wit that most congressmen were afraid of him. Clad in riding clothes and boots and carrying a whip, he would stride into the House, followed by his hunting dogs. On one occasion he hit a dignified member of Congress with his cane in defense of his dogs. One of the congressmen wrote that the new Speaker, Clay, had given universal satisfaction. "Not even Randolph himself has yet attempted to embarrass him," he reported. *"Mr. R. has brought his dog into the House only once this Session* and then the Speaker immediately ordered the Doorkeeper to take her out." When the haughty Virginian tried to engage in a long harangue on a resolution he introduced opposing war with England, Clay called him to order and effectively muzzled him.

To this first session of the House of Representatives over which Clay presided there was elected a group of War Hawks, young men, chiefly from the West and the South, who advocated a declaration of war against Great Britain. Animated by a sense of patriotism and regard for the nation's honor, they resented the arrogant treatment of American sailors and the violation of American maritime rights by Great Britain. Some of them, particularly Richard Mentor Johnson of Kentucky, were stimulated to martial fervor by a belief that the British in Canada had given aid and encouragement to Indian attacks on the northern frontier. Several of the most prominent of the war advocates — Clay, Calhoun, Lowndes, Cheves, Grundy, and Bibb — boarded at the same tavern and ate together. Here they concerted their measures to bring on a declaration of war and were accordingly dubbed "the War Mess."

An economic depression which had hit the staple-exporting states of the Mississippi Valley and the South Atlantic seaboard aided the War Hawks in their agitation. In urging war against Great Britain, Clay did not hesitate to use the appeal to the material interests of Americans as well as to their sense of honor and pride. Speaking to Congress on December 31, 1811, he declared that Great Britain was jealous of the growing economic strength of the United States, which she regarded as a formidable rival. "She sickens at your prosperity," he said.

Although expansionist sentiment had some influence

on the declaration of war, the Clay papers do not indicate that it was important. Rather, they tend to strengthen the view that the war was brought about by resentment of Americans against Great Britain for her violations of our neutral rights and the impressment of our seamen. As early as January, 1806, Clay wrote to Attorney General John Breckinridge that Kentuckians were anxious to know whether war with Great Britain would occur. Such a war, he thought, would be popular in the West. "Perhaps this is a fortunate moment," he observed, "to repress European Aggression and to evince to the world that Americans appreciate their rights in such a way as will induce them, when violated, to engage in war with alacrity and effect." In an oratorical flourish in 1811 he had spoken of Kentuckians capturing Canada, but two years later he protested in a private letter that when "the war was commenced, Canada was not the end but the means, the object of the war being the redress of injuries."

Clay, thirty-four years of age and older than most of the War Hawks, was their guiding spirit. His position as Speaker gave him extraordinary opportunities to advance the cause of the war party. In his selection of the committees of the House he appointed War Hawks to strategic chairmanships. The elder statesmen of the Republican party, on the other hand, particularly President Madison and Albert Gallatin, knowing how poorly prepared the country was for war, tried to restrain the martial zeal of "Young America." But Clay as Speaker proved more influential in formulating policy than President Madison, whom he regarded as a timid soul.

Clay was elated when on June 18, 1812, the United States declared war against Great Britain. The decision was a victory for the War Hawks over the elder statesmen, in a sense, a victory of feeling over reason. More than any other individual, "Harry of the West" was responsible. His emotional oratory and his parliamentary skill substantially affected the direction of public opinion which ruled Congressional action. Americans of his generation were more susceptible to speeches and to personal leadership than later. Nevertheless, the forces that brought the United States into war with Great Britain were far stronger than the agitation of a dynamic leader, even of Clay's stature, or the pressure of a group such as the War Hawks. An accumulation of grievances, a "running account" against Great Britain, had eventuated in war.

At no period of Clay's life did he represent more truly the feeling of the West than at this time. Yet his leadership of the war forces in 1811-1812 was rather atypical than characteristic of the main trend of his life. Throughout most of his career the "Western Star" was a man of peace who exerted himself to prevent foreign wars and to reduce internal friction that threatened civil war. Despite the fact that he was on occasions fiery of speech and that he fought two duels, he was essentially unwarlike; he did not even handle firearms in hunting, the recreation of so many Southern planters and farmers. Possessing no military record himself with which to dazzle the electorate, he strongly disapproved of electing military heroes to public office.

The course of the war brought much humiliation to the American people and especially to Clay, who had confidently predicted easy victory. After Hull's surrender of Detroit, Clay exerted pressure on Secretary of War Monroe to appoint William Henry Harrison to the command of the American forces in the West. Deeply chagrined by successive defeats of American arms, he declared in private letters that President Madison was "wholly unfit for the storms of war."

It is a commentary on the amateur conception of war

that prevailed in the Republic that President Madison at this critical moment considered appointing Clay to the command of the American armies. Even more revealing of the amateur spirit was the fantastic correspondence between General Harrison and Clay in the summer of 1812. On August 29 Harrison wrote to Clay from Cincinnati that his army was "in spirit equal to any that Greece or Rome ever boasted of, but destitute of artillery, of many necessary equipments, and absolutely ignorant of every military evolution." On the following day he dispatched, as if in a panic, another letter to the Kentucky politician asking him to come to his camp to consult with him on the course of operations for the army. Clay had been responsible for getting him and the country into this mess and ought to extricate them from it: "for God's sake, then, come on to Piqua as quickly as possible, and let us endeavor to throw off from the administration that weight of reproach which the late disasters will heap upon them."

As the power of Congress during the war was subordinated to that of the executive, Clay's influence declined. His most important contribution was to the realm of public morale. When Josiah Quincy expressed in Congress the bitter opposition of the New England Federalists to the war policy, Clay replied in a notable speech, delivered on January 8 and 9, 1813, in which he proclaimed the duty of protecting "the gallant tars" of our merchant marine. In expressing this sentiment he truly represented the feeling of most Westerners and Southerners, who were willing to fight to defend the personal rights of American citizens, although few impressed seamen came from their sections.

President Madison was anxious to conclude hostilities that promised little glory for American arms. Accordingly, he jumped at an opportunity for peace negotiations initiated by the Czar of Russia. The British rejected the Czar's offer of mediation but agreed to direct negotiations. In January, 1814, the President appointed Clay one of five commissioners to represent the United States in negotiating a treaty of peace with Great Britain.

Clay reached Ghent on June 28, but the American commissioners had to wait for over a month before the British representatives appeared. The Americans made the mistake of renting a house and living together during the conference. In their daily association the contrasting personalities of the group caused friction. John Quincy Adams, an introspective New Englander who was an early riser and read five chapters of the Bible every morning before breakfast, disapproved of the hedonistic ways of some of his colleagues, particularly of the extroverted Kentuckian. He withdrew from the common dining table because he did not like to see them drink bad wine and smoke cigars and waste time after dinner. He was annoyed at the late hours that Clay kept in gambling. Often the company in Clay's room would leave just as Adams was rising. Yet the New Englander noted in his diary that on several occasions he himself had played cards — all fours and whist — with the genial Kentuckian and some of the ladies of Ghent. Gallatin was usually the peacemaker in family squabbles.

For more than four and a half months the British and the Americans struggled to negotiate a peace treaty. The American representatives were at a great disadvantage, for Napoleon's army defending Paris was defeated in the spring and thus released Great Britain's energies for the American war. The British commissioners acted as though they were dealing with a defeated country and incensed the Americans by demanding a cession of United States territory for a vast Indian reservation. During the greater part of the negotiations Clay and his fellow commissioners were chiefly employed in rejecting disgraceful terms of peace proposed by the British.

Clay's attitude toward the issue of impressment throws a curious light on his personality. The original instructions to the American commissioners required that they should make no treaty that did not contain a renunciation by Great Britain of her claim to impress American seamen on United States ships. Clay wrote to W. H. Crawford just after reaching Ghent that if it were necessary for the United States to forgo this demand in order to obtain peace, he would be willing to violate instructions. The stipulation that the British renounce impressment of American seamen, he argued, had become "a mere theoretic pretension" since the practical evil had ceased. The Secretary of State canceled the stipulations in the instructions on impressment and neutral rights after Gallatin had advised him to do so. Yet Adams noted in his diary on November 4 that at a meeting of the American mission, "Mr. Clay, of all the members, had alone been urgent to present an article stipulating the abolition of the practice of impressment." The commissioners finally acceded to his demand. Throughout the negotiations Clay advocated playing the Western card game of brag and of calling what he thought was the enemy's bluff. When the treaty was signed, however, it contained no renunciation by the British of the odious practice of impressment.

Clay and Adams clashed frequently. Although their temperaments seemed antithetical, Adams thought that of the members of the commission Clay was most like himself. "There is the same dogmatical, overbearing manner," he observed, "the same harshness of look and expression, and the same forgetfulness of the courtesies of society in both. An impartial person judging between them I think would say that one has the strongest, the other the most cultivated understanding; that one has the most ardency, the other the most experience of mankind; that one has a mind most gifted by nature, the other a mind less cankered by prejudice."

Their principal disagreement was over the surrender to the British of the right to navigate the Mississippi in return for the privilege of New England fishermen to fish in Canadian waters and to dry their catch on unpopulated islands in the vicinity. Clay argued that the war had canceled the right of the British to the navigation of the Mississippi granted by the treaty of 1783. He believed that Adams, in his zeal to obtain fishing rights for New England, disregarded the interests of the Western states. The right to navigate the Mississippi was immensely more valuable than the fishing right. Contemptuously he said during one of the discussions that the surrender of the exclusive control of the Mississippi was much too high a price for "the mere liberty of drying fish upon a desert." The navigation privilege, he believed, would be an entering wedge for British traders to traffic with American Indians and to exert a dangerous influence over them. Clay declared that he would never sign a treaty giving the British that right "so help him God to keep him steady to his purpose." Adams observed that he spoke this sentiment in a "harsh, angry, and overbearing tone," which the New Englander attributed to "the involuntary effusion of a too positive temper."

Clay, indeed, was very unhappy over the turn that the treaty negotiations took. He thought that Gallatin and Bayard were too eager for peace and too yielding to the insolent demands of the British. On December 14, ten days before a treaty was finally negotiated, he spoke despondently of his fear that the Americans would make a "damned bad treaty" and he did not know whether he would sign it. When the British finally accepted the

American proposals that the treaty be silent on the rights of navigating the Mississippi and the fisheries, he was so chagrined that he talked of breaking off negotiations. He was for continuing the war, so Adams reported, three years longer rather than for the United States to come out of the war with a loss of honor. Nevertheless, he finally signed the peace treaty with the other commissioners on December 24. But there was a last bit of fireworks when Clay lost his temper because Adams wished to retain the custodianship of the papers and records of the negotiation of the treaty before turning them over to the State Department.

After the conclusion of the treaty Clay remained in Europe with Adams and Gallatin to negotiate a commercial agreement with Great Britain. He was reluctant to go to London until he heard of Jackson's glorious victory of New Orleans on January 8. Then he felt he could hold up his head with pride as he faced the British. The tedious negotiations gained the United States some privileges but failed to open up the West India trade. By May 10, Clay was "sick of Europe, and sicker of European politics," and longed to return to America. Actually, however, he did not arrive in this country until September, 1815.

In retrospect Clay counted many gains from his experiences in Europe. He was paid a total of sixteen thousand five hundred dollars for his expenses and salary, out of which he was able to invest through Baring Brothers approximately forty-five hundred dollars in the 6 per cent bonds of the United States. He had met European statesmen and intellectuals. His stay in Europe, nevertheless, had made him even more enthusiastically American than before he crossed the Atlantic. At Ghent he had thought that the United States had concluded a bad treaty, but after his return he developed a more favorable view of it. He spoke with pride of the United States' achievement in the war. She had fought, he boasted, the most powerful nation in the world and had proved that a democracy could be victorious in war. Above all, the United States had restored its own self-respect and gained the respect of Europe. This young country was no longer subservient to Great Britain or submissive to European insults and aggression, but had won "a Second War for American Independence."

In one of his earliest speeches in Congress after returning from Ghent, Clay sought to stir national pride and patriotism among his countrymen. Critics had said that the War of 1812 was a useless conflict and they had opposed a direct tax to pay the war debt as well as a bill to keep the United States strong by supporting an adequate standing army and a navy. In rebuking them Clay pointed out the wisdom of maintaining a strong standing army and he took occasion to point out the national benefits from war against Great Britain. One of the intangible gains was the awakened spirit of patriotism and the valor shown by our soldiers and sailors. The glory won by Jackson, Hull of the *Constitution*, Lawrence, and Perry did not end, he pointed out, with their heroic acts but would continue to animate the country "in the hour of peril hereafter." He asked, "Did the battle of Thermopylae preserve Greece but once?"

Critics had complained that the United States had made an inglorious treaty since it did not force Great Britain to renounce the right of impressment. Clay replied that British aggression had ended before the ratification of the treaty, and Great Britain would never again attempt to encroach upon the United States' rights by renewing the odious practice. If she ever did, he declared, he for one would take up arms again to resist her. In this speech he laid down a broad program of nationalism —

maintenance of a strong army and navy, federal aid to internal improvements so that a chain of turnpike roads and canals would extend from Canada to New Orleans and intersect the mountains, and a protective tariff to encourage American manufactures. Thus "Harry of the West" struck the keynote of a new period that the United States was entering and a new phase of his own political career.

I I I

A New Type of Republican

THE KEYNOTE to Clay's political career in the decade after his return from Ghent was that of optimistic nationalism. In this critical decade of his life Clay changed the emphasis of his political thinking from the preservation of human rights to the advancement of the material well-being of his section and the nation. He became a strong ally of the greatest business corporation in America, the Second Bank of the United States. He stoutly fought for the material development of the West by construction of internal improvements with federal aid. He laid the foundations of his reputation as a compromiser in achieving the second Missouri Compromise. His economic nationalism also emerged in this decade, especially in the advocacy of the American System. Indeed, he became a new type of Republican, whom Thomas Jefferson would hardly have recognized as one of his former henchmen.

After the War of 1812 the Federalist party was prostrate and the Republican party, virtually lacking opposition, developed two factions — the Old, or State Rights, group, and the New, or National, Republicans. Clay took his position in the camp of the "New Republicans," who thought of the federal government in a positive role and who saw the need of interpreting the Constitution liberally. The War of 1812 contributed something to this changed attitude; the growth of the country subtly produced new attitudes toward national power; and the economic distress that followed the panic of 1819 gave added impulse to the growth of democracy. Clay was sensitive to the new currents and he easily discarded the old trammels of constitutional interpretation that hampered the growth of the young nation.

On January 8, 1816, John C. Calhoun, then as strong a nationalist as Clay, made a report to Congress recommending the immediate chartering of a Second Bank of the United States. In supporting this measure the Kentucky Senator made a remarkable speech reversing the stand he had taken before the war. A national bank was now needed to correct the chaotic condition of the currency and the proposed charter would safeguard the institution from foreign control.

After the bill had become law Clay sought to reap personal advantages from it. He used his influence to get branches established at Lexington and Louisville and wrote to President William Jones suggesting the names of prominent people in Lexington to serve as directors of the local branch. He advised that since Lexington was strongly Republican in politics a majority of such directors should be Republicans. Eager to make money, he tried to rent a building that he owned to the bank for its Lexington branch. Also he sought to become one of the national directors of the bank, buying five shares of its stock in order to qualify himself for the position. Although he was not appointed at this time, he was offered the coveted position in 1818. However, he then declined the appointment, explaining that legislation affecting the bank might come before Congress and that in such a contingency he did not wish to appear biased in favor of the great financial monopoly. Nevertheless, he assured the president that he was a warm friend of the institution.

Clay did establish a profitable connection with the bank during the following year as one of its attorneys. He served as attorney for the bank in its controversy with the state of Ohio over the taxation of its Ohio branch. It was a great triumph to win his case, Osborn *versus* the Bank of the United States, in the Supreme Court of the United States. As agent for the bank in Kentucky and Ohio, he prosecuted debtors who had defaulted, notably the powerful Congressman Richard Mentor Johnson and his brother. He was liberally rewarded for his services, receiving a retaining fee of $6000 annually. But there was an enormous number of the bank's cases on docket in Kentucky and Ohio, approximately four hundred, Clay reported to President Langdon Cheves on February 10, 1821. Clay was financially embarrassed at this period of his life, and he was grateful for the stipend from the bank.

Throughout his championship of the interests of the bank he claimed that he was seeking only equal treatment and justice for his client, not special privileges. After the panic of 1819, when the bank had to call in many of its loans and foreclose mortgages, it became very unpopular in the West. Clay's connection with this great financial institution apparently did not alienate the masses. A considerable number of the debtors to the bank in Ohio whom Clay had prosecuted as attorney voted for him in the presidential election of 1824.

In 1817 Clay warmly supported Calhoun's Bonus bill, providing a fund to construct national roads and canals. The bill passed Congress, but Madison on his last day as President vetoed it and his successor, James Monroe, in his first message to Congress proclaimed his belief that the Constitution did not give Congress the authority to engage in internal improvements. Clay challenged this narrow interpretation, for, representing the interests of a West that needed desperately to get out of the mud and to obtain roads to the Eastern markets, he perceived the need of advocating a liberal interpretation of the Constitution. In a brilliant speech on March 13, 1818, he argued that the Constitution gave to Congress the authority to appropriate money for internal improvements and furthermore that it was desirable for the legislature of a growing young country to make such appropriations. He foresaw the great expansion of the United States and the need to interpret the Constitution liberally in order for the government to keep pace with this growth and to advance the general welfare.

Clay's ambition to become President seems to have decidedly affected his relations with President Monroe. In 1817 the latter appointed John Quincy Adams to the office of Secretary of State, which in this period was regarded as a steppingstone to the Presidency. Clay appears to have been greatly disappointed and declined the War Department and the mission to England, both of which were offered him. Afterwards he did not spare the venerated elder statesman of his party. Jefferson in 1818 condemned the Kentucky politician for "rallying an opposition to the administration," which he implied was motivated by personal ambition. Such conduct, he observed, would only lead to the throwing away of "the distinction and favor in the public eye" that Clay had previously acquired.

One of the clashes between the President and the high-mettled Speaker arose over the proper policy in regard to Florida. In 1810 while Clay was in the Senate he had expressed the expansionist spirit of the West in a speech upholding President Madison's proclamation extending the boundary of Louisiana to the Perdido River, thereby absorbing West Florida. In this speech he clearly revealed his desire for the United States to acquire East Florida also. Nine years later, however, he appeared to have lost his enthusiasm for the quick acquisition of this peninsula, for he severely criticized the Monroe administration for its negotiation of a treaty with Spain to buy this province.

Clay's chief objection was that the treaty surrendered the claim of the United States to Texas as far as the Rio Grande. This claim was debatable, dating to the purchase in 1803 of the Louisiana territory with its indefinite western boundaries. When Spain delayed ratification Clay argued in 1820 that the treaty had lapsed and should not be renewed. He took the position that the acquisition of Florida would not be equivalent to the surrender of Texas. He wished the United States to recognize the "Patriots" — American citizens in East Florida who were rebelling against Spanish rule — and at the same time to assert its claims in Texas to the fullest extent. He maintained that the occupation of Texas would not produce a war with Spain and that Florida would eventually become American territory without effort on the part of the United States Government. Monroe's policy rather than Clay's prevailed, however, and in February, 1821, Spain after much procrastination surrendered Florida to the United States, which in turn gave up its claims to Texas.

It was at this period that Clay made one of his most eloquent and flamboyant speeches, one that delighted the galleries but injured him. In the spring of 1818 General Jackson had crossed the boundary line into Florida in pursuit of marauding Seminole Indians, had seized two Spanish towns, and had executed two British subjects and several hostile Indian chiefs. Clay presumed the step was taken without authority, for if the President had actually authorized the invasion, "the Constitutional provision is a dead letter which confides to Congress the power of declaring war." Clay strongly supported the resolutions of censure of the general introduced into the House of Representatives.

When it was known that he would speak on this exciting subject, the Senate adjourned to listen to the great orator and the galleries were crowded with ladies and gentlemen, for a Clay oration was great entertainment to this generation. Clay spoke extemporaneously. The recorded speech was solemn and dignified, but Mrs. Samuel Harrison Smith, who was one of the audience, wrote that Mr. Clay was not only eloquent on this occasion, but amusing, and "more than once made the whole house laugh." During his three-day oration, gallant gentlemen refreshed the ladies in the gallery by handing oranges up to them attached by handkerchiefs to long poles. When the orator met Mrs. Smith on the first day of his speech he apologized to her that he had not spoken longer, offering as his excuse that his voice gave out, for he had begun in too loud a tone and had soon exhausted himself.

In this philippic Clay declared that the main cause of the Seminole War was the extremely harsh and unjust Indian treaty of 1814 which Jackson had extorted from the Creeks and Seminoles. He disclaimed any hostility to Jackson or Monroe, but he desired that military insubordination be rebuked. Echoing a famous speech of Patrick Henry, who had come from his native Hanover County, Clay said, "Remember that Greece had her Alexander, Rome her Caesar, England her Cromwell, France her Bonaparte, and that if we would escape the rock on which they split we must avoid their errors." Although Clay's speech was eloquent and characterized by humanity and sound principles he had not carefully checked some of the facts used in his indictment. His speech incurred the hostility of Jackson, who seldom forgot a personal attack. Monroe's friends also resented the speech, which contributed to the widening gulf between the President and the Speaker. A movement to deprive Clay of the speakership was nevertheless opposed by Monroe partly because the Kentuckian was an outstanding representative of the West.

Clay clashed with the President also over the timing of the recognition of the South American republics. As early as 1816 he expressed the belief that the United States should intervene in behalf of the patriots of South America to stop a bloody and cruel war. He declared that the release of any part of America from the dominion of the Old World added to the general security of the New. His remarks foreshadowed one of the basic ideas of the Monroe Doctrine, the curbing of foreign influence in the Western Hemisphere.

President Monroe opposed a precipitate recognition of the South American republics. He was anxious not to endanger the delicate negotiations for the purchase of Florida. Clay, on the other hand, on March 24, 1818, made a motion to recognize the Republic of La Plata by appropriating $18,000 for the salary and outfit for a minister to that country. He also concerted with the representative of the Buenos Aires government at Washington to force the United States to abandon its neutral policy. But Congress sustained the cautious policy of the President and of Secretary of State John Quincy Adams by voting overwhelmingly against Clay's resolution.

Although Clay's advocacy of the cause of the South American republics probably was intertwined with his personal ambitions, he was combining a great public service with attention to his own personal welfare. On this occasion Clay seems to have been primarily motivated not by a factious opposition to the President or by ambition, but by genuine sympathy for a people struggling for their liberty. In this feeling he was spokesman for Kentucky, whose legislature by a resolution at this time advocated the recognition by the United States of the independence of the Spanish colonies in America. Perhaps also Kentucky's interest in South American independence was partly based on a hope for the expansion of Mississippi Valley trade with the new countries.

In a speech of March 24 and 28, Clay argued persuasively for the recognition of the Latin-American republics. He frankly admitted that there were selfish as well as altruistic reasons why the United States should take the lead. The development of trade was attractive. Furthermore, it was established American policy to recognize *de facto* governments and the United Provinces of the Río de la Plata had established a stable government. There was little danger of a war with Spain. The people of South America were not too ignorant or superstitious to govern themselves; their struggle for independence was like the American Revolution. Indeed Clay was a humanitarian and a lover of liberty who believed that it was the mission of the United States to advance the cause of liberty throughout the world.

In making this notable speech Clay did not expect Congress to adopt his motion, for "the whole weight of the executive" was opposed. His purpose was rather "to awaken public attention to the great struggle to the South." In this he succeeded. He also sought to obtain accurate knowledge of the condition and resources of the South American countries and to report such information to the American people. Monroe's administration finally recognized the South American republics in 1822. Clay's advocacy of their cause was one of his public acts which gave him greatest satisfaction to the end of his life.

He remains today one of the most highly regarded American statesmen in the Latin-American countries.

In the fall of 1821 Clay resigned from Congress. Financial difficulties made it necessary for him to return to his law practice. He had gambled to some extent during his stay in Washington, losing and then winning back in one evening eight thousand dollars to the dissolute Congressman George Poindexter. Such revels reduced his energies but did not seriously impair his financial standing. More important was the failure of a friend whose note he had endorsed, which left him in debt for a large sum to the Bank of the United States. In any case long service in Congress entailed a considerable monetary sacrifice.

Facile though he was before a criminal jury, Clay was an exceptionally able lawyer in civil cases. His opinions given to the United States Bank officials, for example, show good judgment, insight into human nature, and excellent reasoning ability. The esteem in which he was held led to his appointment by the legislature in 1821 to represent the state in a dispute with Virginia over land titles within Kentucky. But the legal profession did not appeal to the ambitious Kentuckian, and as soon as he had restored his finances he decided to return to politics. In December, 1823, he again took his seat in Congress, where he was re-elected Speaker.

In this term, his last in the House of Representatives, he spoke vigorously in behalf of Western interests. After Monroe had in May, 1822, vetoed a bill for repairing the Cumberland Road, Clay urged Congress to appropriate $30,000 for the survey of roads and canals that the President might consider valuable for military defense, post roads, or national interest. Since Monroe had recently attacked the constitutionality of the use of federal funds for internal improvements, Clay devoted the greater part of his speech to the argument that the Constitution should be interpreted in the light of its purpose of creating a stronger Union. He envisaged a rapidly expanding country that would need a network of roads and canals; "this government," he orated, "is to last, I trust, forever; we may at least hope it will endure until the wave of population, cultivation, and intelligence shall have washed the Rocky Mountains and have mingled with the Pacific." He cited the improvement of Mississippi navigation, and the upkeep and extension of the Cumberland Road (both of primary benefit to the West) as two examples of the necessity of national rather than state action in executing internal improvement projects that were essentially national in scope.

Clay's greatest effort during his last term in the House of Representatives, one of the most significant of his life, was his two-day speech on American industry on March 30 and 31, 1824. This speech was not an oratorical flourish but was based on numerous statistics and facts to show the desirability of increasing the protective tariff. He began by a gloomy description of the economic depression of the country, which, he said, was indicated by many symptoms including "the ravenous pursuit after public situations, not for the sake of honors and the performance of their public duties, but as a means of private subsistence." He attributed this depression to the drying up of the European markets after the Napoleonic Wars. The obvious remedy was the development of a home market by protecting American manufacturers with a tariff. Although Clay had been an Anglophobe, in this speech he praised the economic greatness of the British Isles, which he attributed to their use of machinery and a protective tariff policy. Clay admitted that the Americans would always "be an agricultural people," yet an expanding American industry would lessen the competition

among farmers by draining some of the agricultural population to the city.

Point by point he rebutted the arguments of those opposed to the increase of the tariff. The protective tariff was
constitutional; it would free the United States from foreign dependence in time of war; it would not decrease
the revenue of the government nor diminish navigation
since increased coast-wide trade would compensate for the
loss of foreign trade. Nor would the interests of the
Southern states be injured. The tariff would encourage
the growth of American textile factories, which would furnish a home market for Southern cotton, and the South itself could go into manufacturing, while farmers could
profit from furnishing provisions to artisans. Clay appealed to the patriotism of the country to establish an
American economy, and he urged that the spirit of compromise prevail between regional and class interests in
working out a practical solution of a tariff policy. The
speech was one of the best cases for a protective tariff
ever made in the United States, and became the classic argument for the policy of protection.

Clay was, in effect, advocating a planned national economy through legislative interference. From Madison,
whom he regarded as the greatest American statesman
after Washington, he received a letter of moderate dissent. The Virginia statesman favored a natural economy
except for the production of articles necessary for national defense. Clay could not persuade the Southerners,
who were principally exporters and consumers, that their
interests would be promoted by a higher protective tariff.
The great interest of America, and especially of the South,
was the consumer interest, which a high tariff seemed to
injure. Clay, therefore, was never able to get the South to
support him for President. He had to depend on seeking a
Northwestern and Northeastern alliance.

Clay had strong economic and local reasons for championing his "American System," which was designed to build a more self-sufficient economy by means of a protective tariff and federal aid for internal improvements. Kentucky's main staple, hemp, required tariff protection for survival. The Hart family and Clay himself were producers of hemp. Clay had earlier made an adventure of capital in becoming a partner in the Madison Hemp and Flax Spinning Company. The Tariff Act of 1824 imposed a duty of 4½ cents per square yard on bagging cloth for cotton bales, a provision designed to favor the Lexington factories. But the cotton producing states protested against it as contrived "to enrich Mr. Clay's Kentucky pets." In the 1840's Clay's economic interests were involved in a high tariff policy, for his son Thomas Hart was engaged in manufacturing cotton bagging and hemp rope. The father lent him a large sum to provide capital for this business and the old statesman actually served as agent to sell his son's goods. Furthermore, Clay had close friends and relatives who were sugar planters in Louisiana, and Louisiana sugar desperately needed protection.

Nevertheless, Clay's advocacy of the American System was more than crude economic self-interest. Van Buren in his autobiography expresses the opinion that Clay was sincere in his confidence in the soundness and value of a protective tariff, but that it was doubtful whether Clay's long championship of such legislation was more a liability than an asset in his career. Clay's belief in the wisdom of the protective tariff policy was not merely a catering to vested interests but was a part of his broad nationalism, a patriotic desire to see his country become strong and self-sufficient. He saw only the benign aspects of the rise of American industry under the patronage of the protective tariff, not the exploitation of human labor.

Clay's American System was a beautifully integrated and harmonious system of political economy on paper. It was simplicity itself. The two leading elements were a protective tariff to encourage American industry and furnish a home market for the agricultural products of the American farmer, and federal appropriations for internal improvements. It envisaged a great development of internal trade between the sections, justifying the construction of internal improvements at federal expense. Its collateral elements were the establishment of a strong United States bank, which would insure a stable currency to facilitate intersectional trade, and a land bill giving to the states the proceeds from the sale of the public land to finance internal improvement projects. The system was like a well-oiled and perfectly adjusted machine, each part of which was indispensable to the proper functioning of the whole. Clay's land policy, for example, would deprive the federal government of much of its revenue, thereby preventing a surplus from accumulating in the treasury as a result of the operation of a protective tariff.

The American System, too, had the element of flexibility, for when manufactures had taken firm root, he pointed out, duties could be reduced. Later, as a presidential candidate, he maintained for the benefit of Southerners that he favored a tariff for revenue, with discriminations in the schedules in behalf of American industry. But low tariffs, he said, would lead to a flood of foreign importations which would have the disastrous effect of draining the country of specie.

In 1824 Clay was forty-seven years old, at the prime of his intellectual development. His career had been an unvaried succession of victories and his correspondence expressed a great optimism as to his future. One office of leadership, that of governor, he had not won, nor did he ever seriously seek it, for his predominant interest was in national politics. Like his contemporary, Calhoun, he devoted little attention to social reform in the state, to free schools or care of the handicapped and underprivileged. Nor did he later exert himself to promote the railroad development of Kentucky.

Since his return from Ghent his political philosophy had subtly changed so that his enemies had grounds to accuse him of adopting the ideas of the old Federalist party. John Quincy Adams somewhat later recalled that Clay had risen "upon the broadest shoulders of democracy. But his European expedition tinged both his principles and his deportment with Aristocracy — perhaps to the improvement of his character, but to the loss of his standing with the Democracy." Actually, Clay's matured political philosophy was an amalgam of Jeffersonian and Federalist principles. He had little sympathy with the Federalist scorn of the common man. Nor did he agree with their opposition to the territorial expansion of the nation. But he accepted the progressive elements of their program, namely, a flexible interpretation of the Constitution and a belief that the federal government should play a positive role in the economic development of the nation.

I V

A Fateful Decision

NOT ONCE, but on several occasions, a turn of ill luck mocked the ambitions, the human affections, and the passionate hopes of Henry Clay. His life exhibited some of the characteristics of a Greek drama in which an essentially noble character is brought low by a human defect. The Achilles' heel of Clay's nature was his craving for high public office. The first great blow to his political aspirations came in the presidential election of 1824. Following that event he faced a great dilemma and made a fatal decision.

Yet "Gallant Harry" was a man of a remarkably resilient nature. When a blow of fate struck him he soon recovered and could contemplate with keen delight the green lawns, the trees, the flocks, and herds of the Kentucky countryside, which he called "this paradise of a country." Harriet Martineau, an English intellectual, conversed with Clay in 1835 and found that the frustrations in his career had left him philosophic rather than bitter and disillusioned. "Mr. Clay," she wrote, "is a man of an irritable and impetuous nature, over which he has obtained a truly noble mastery. His moderation is now his most striking characteristic."

In the presidential election of 1824 several aggressive politicians aspired to the place held so long by "the Virginia dynasty." John C. Calhoun was the youngest, forty-two years old. But after the Pennsylvania legislature declared itself for Jackson, he decided to lower his ambition temporarily and became a candidate for Vice President. William H. Crawford, Secretary of the Treasury and an astute politician, was also a formidable contender until he suffered a paralytic stroke. He was nominated by the Congressional caucus, but this support proved a handicap, for the rising democratic sentiment of the period was hostile to this method of selecting presidential candidates. The best educated of the candidates was John Quincy Adams, Monroe's Secretary of State, who could count on the support of New England.

Andrew Jackson, fifty-seven years old, presented a serious threat to Clay's prospects because he was a military hero and his candidacy would divide the vote of the West. Clay did not take Jackson very seriously, however, believing that Adams would be his strongest competitor. He could never understand why a military hero could capture the imagination and win the votes of the masses for President.

John Quincy Adams felt that Clay would be a dangerous competitor for the office of President. Being "the first distinguished man that the Western country has presented as a statesman to the Union," he wrote in his diary, "they are profoundly proud of him." He pronounced Clay to be "only half educated," loose in morals, impetuous in temper, with very popular manners, and adept in political management. He admitted, however, that Clay was an eloquent man and that he had "large and liberal views of public affairs." He predicted that if the Kentuckian should be elected President, "his administration would be a perpetual succession of intrigue and management with the legislature," and would sacrifice Eastern interests to those of the Western country and the slaveholders.

In the interest of his candidacy "Harry of the West" wrote many letters to politicians in the different states. While he encouraged them to act in his behalf, he told them that he would make no deals or promises to win the Presidency, for he was determined that if elected he should enter office with a pure conscience, untrammeled and uncommitted. He had a warm supporter in Senator Josiah S. Johnston of Louisiana, a Transylvania University graduate, who served informally as his campaign manager. He kept in frequent correspondence with other political leaders, particularly Peter B. Porter in New York; John Sergeant in Pennsylvania; and Judge Francis Brooke of Fredricksburg, Virginia.

Clay was wistful to win the support of his native state, Virginia. He sought to propagate the idea in Virginia that Crawford, also a Virginian by birth, had no chance of election and that he himself was the only candidate from the slaveholding states whom the Northwestern states would vote for. Clay realized that his views on the tariff and internal improvements were a handicap in the South. "You will oppose my election I suppose in Virginia," he wrote to Judge Brooke. "I have no right to complain. . . . You will oppose me because I think that the interests of all parts of the Union should be taken care of, that the interests of the interior, on the two subjects mentioned, as well as that of the maritime coast, ought to be provided for." He tried to show that the growth of an interior since the formation of the Constitution required a changed outlook on governmental problems.

An unvarying characteristic of Clay was his optimism, which gave him confidence in all his campaigns that he would be victorious. He failed to gauge the rising democratic sentiment of the country and to place himself at the head of it, as his rival Jackson did. In the election of 1824 he felt sure that he would win with the vote of the West and the middle states. If the election went to the House of Representatives he was confident of obtaining a majority vote of the state delegations.

Yet he was far from the mark. He failed to persuade Crawford to retire. Instead of winning the entire Western vote, he shared it with Jackson. He made strenuous efforts to attract the Eastern states outside of New England to his support by circulating campaign material prepared by the Kentucky Committee of Correspondence. His rivals, however, injured his prospects in this area by circulating rumors that he had withdrawn from the race. All during the campaign, also, Clay suffered from ill health and could not exert himself in directing the efforts of his supporters. When the electoral votes were counted in November, Jackson led the list with ninety-nine, Adams came second with eighty-four, Crawford third with forty-one, and Clay last with thirty-seven votes. "The Western Star" had won the support of only three states, Kentucky, Ohio, and Missouri. Since no candidate had obtained a majority, the election was transferred to the House of Representatives.

It was ironic that chance, to which the Kentuckian had always confidently trusted, should have played him false on this crucial occasion. A gig overturned on the miserable roads of Louisiana, injuring two Clay supporters on their way to the legislature so that they were unable to attend. These legislators and two others who failed to reach the capital in time for the vote for presidential electors might have tipped the scales in favor of "Harry of the West" in the close election in that state. If he had won the vote of Louisiana, he would have become one of the three candidates eligible to be voted upon in the House of Representatives and would have had an excellent chance of winning. Clay also seems to have been deprived of enough votes in the New York balloting through trickery and bad faith to prevent him from tying with Crawford for third place, which, independently of the vote in Louisiana, would have made him a candidate in the House election.

After his elimination in the electoral college, Clay found himself in one of the most difficult situations of his life. His influence in the House might determine the presidential election. In January, 1825, he was courted by each faction, but refused to commit himself publicly until the latter part of that month. Since Crawford was physically unable to serve as President, Clay considered only Adams and Jackson. Of the two he preferred Adams because the election of the New Englander, he believed, would not "inflict any wound upon the character of our institutions." The elevation of Jackson to the Presidency, on the other hand, he feared, "would give to the military spirit a stimulus and confidence that might lead to the most pernicious results."

Clay did not make his decision without weighing the effects of his choice upon his own political career. Since Ohio would be likely to support Adams, he observed, a vote for Jackson by Kentucky would divide "our friends" and at the same time not prevent Adams's election. "My friends," he wrote, "entertain the belief that their kind wishes toward me will in the end be more likely to be accomplished by so bestowing their votes [on Adams]."

Before Clay had revealed his decision as to whom he would support in the House election, several of his friends visited John Quincy Adams, notably Congressmen Robert Letcher of Kentucky and John Scott of Missouri. They both denied that they came as emissaries from the Kentucky statesman but they told Adams that the appointment of Clay to a cabinet post would please Clay's friends in the

West. Adams realized clearly what lay back of their words and he wrote in his diary after a conversation with Letcher *"Incedo super ignes* [I am treading upon coals of fire]." Although he made no promises to appoint Clay Secretary of State if elected, he virtually told them that if he were elected by the votes of the West he would appoint a Western man to his cabinet. Despite his New England conscience Adams made not one but several implicit bargains with influential congressmen from crucial states.

On January 7, the Kentucky legislature instructed its delegation in Congress to vote for Jackson for President. Within a few days after the instruction had arrived, Clay had a conference with Adams to ascertain the position of the New England candidate on major national questions. Adams must have satisfied him, for the Kentuckian told him at this time that he would cast his vote for him. Although Clay had championed the validity of legislative instruction in 1816, and was later to do so again, he now paid no attention to the wishes of the majority of the legislature. In a speech some years later at Nashville Clay declared that he had not violated the principle of instructions in 1825 because the legislature had no right to instruct him — only his congressional district of Fayette, Woodford, and Jessamine counties possessed the right.

When Clay announced his intention to vote for Adams, the smiles and flatteries of the Jackson partisans turned to bitter denunciations of the "traitor to the West." He was accused, he wrote, of defeating General Jackson's election to leave the Western pretensions open for himself. Clay declared that if he had had a free choice among the able men of the country he would not have selected Adams, but he could not vote for Jackson, a military chieftain. "I cannot believe," he observed, "that killing two thousand five hundred Englishmen at New Orleans qualifies [a person] for the various, difficult, and complicated duties of the chief magistracy."

On January 18, before the election occurred in the House of Representatives, there appeared in the *Columbia Centinel* of Philadelphia a canard that embittered Clay's subsequent career. An anonymous communication from a member of the House of Representatives accused Clay of having entered into a corrupt bargain by which the Kentuckian would cast his vote for Adams in return for the appointment of Secretary of State. The presidential election in the House of Representatives was scheduled for February 9, and this anonymous letter seems to have been a desperate scheme of the Jackson partisans to deter Clay from voting for Adams.

Clay was shocked and outraged by this charge and immediately replied in the *National Intelligencer* of Washington denouncing the writer as a liar and in effect challenging him to a duel. Shortly thereafter a Pennsylvania congressman, George Kremer, published a card admitting his authorship of the first communication and offering to prove the correctness of his allegation. Kremer was an eccentric, a laughingstock in Washington, noted for his overcoat made of leopard skins. When the accuser was revealed, Clay realized that he had made a mistake in challenging him to a duel, for an encounter with Kremer could only be a farce. Accordingly, he now moved that a committee of the House be appointed to investigate the charges. When the committee met, Kremer refused to appear before it, so that no investigation was held. Clay believed, and probably with reason, that Senator John H. Eaton, a crony of Jackson, was the author of the Kremer letter.

On the day of the election Clay and the Kentucky delegation voted for Adams, but the deciding ballot was cast in the New York delegation. The congressmen from this state were so divided that General Stephen Van Rens-selaer, "the last of the Patroons," who had not made up his mind, became the crucial figure. Shortly before the vote in the House of Representatives was taken Clay and Webster frightened him with predictions of danger to men of property should Jackson become President. The old gentleman, who was very devout, closed his eyes and prayed to the Lord to give him guidance on this decisive occasion. When he opened his eyes he saw lying on the floor by his seat a ballot with Adams's name on it. Inter-preting this coincidence as an expression of God's will, he cast his ballot for Adams, thus determining the vote of the New York delegation and deciding the election.

Three days after the election President-elect Adams offered the position of Secretary of State in his cabinet to Henry Clay. The Kentuckian now had to make the most fateful decision of his life. His most influential advisers urged him to accept, pointing out that the West would be disappointed if he did not enter the cabinet, that his rejection of the offer would be a triumph for Kremer and his enemies, and that tenure of the Secretaryship of State would strengthen his claim later to the Presidency. Ac-cordingly, he accepted the position.

Jackson had become convinced of the truth of Kremer's charge and toward the end of February wrote his friend William B. Lewis in Tennessee that Clay was the "Ju-das of the West," who had sold his honor for thirty pieces of silver. He voted with a considerable minority of sena-tors to reject Clay's nomination as Secretary of State. On his way home to Tennessee after the adjournment of Con-gress he made statements to individuals and public gath-erings that the will of the people had been defeated by a corrupt bargain between Adams and Clay. The charge "bargain and corruption" was reiterated by Jackson's fol-lowers and it became a powerful political issue in the presidential campaign of 1828. It dogged Clay in all his subsequent efforts to obtain the Presidency and brought agony into his life. Both John Quincy Adams and Clay denied emphatically that they had made any improper agreement, and the most careful searching of the evidence has turned up nothing to incriminate Clay.

Nonetheless, the charge of a corrupt bargain was too good political capital not to be exploited to the fullest by partisans of Jackson. In the spring of 1827 Jackson was quoted as saying that he had spurned an offer which emissaries of Clay had made in 1825 promising the Presidency if he would commit himself as to a satisfactory appointment of Secretary of State. In the furor that followed, Jackson declared that he had been approached by "a respectable member of Congress" whom he supposed to be an emissary from Clay. The "respectable member" turned out to be James Buchanan of Pennsylvania, who denied making such an offer and whose testimony gave reason to believe that, instead of Clay's being guilty of seeking to bargain, Jackson's friends were the aggressors. On the rebound from this charge Clay published an *Address to the Public* in which he set forth the evidence exonerating himself.

The bitter partisan attacks on his character to which his acceptance of the Secretaryship of State rendered him liable caused Clay untold anguish. He spent much energy in his subsequent career gathering evidence to refute the charges. Ultimately he admitted that he had made a mistake in accepting the appointment, an error which arose, he said, from "underrating the power of detraction and the force of ignorance." The long agony which he suffered over these accusations comes out in a letter written in 1837: "I thank God that I have been permitted to live down those charges," accusations which he rightly ascribed as exploited for political effect. But the charges were renewed with virulence during his campaign for President in 1844.

Clay began his duties as Secretary of State with distaste. "I know my *forte* is the H. of R.," he wrote. "But I will endeavor to do my duty in this new office, and if God grant me life and health, I will disappoint and triumph over my enemies." The duties of the department were too numerous and too incongruous for its limited staff. Its foreign business had greatly increased since the recognition by the United States of the South American republics. Moreover, it handled many subjects later taken care of by the Department of the Interior, such as the granting of patents and copyrights. Clay suggested that Congress should either create a Home Department or increase the number of clerks in the State Department. As early as March 26, 1825, he found his "new office not a bed of roses. But one that requires me to work 12 or 14 hours per day."

He had anticipated that Adams's irascible temper and his faultfinding nature would lead to friction, but he found that he got along very smoothly with the President. He and Adams agreed on the main objectives of the administration. Indeed, Adams's nationalism and his enthusiasm for federal aid for internal improvements even outstripped Clay's. The Secretary of State approved of the leading measures advanced by Adams, including a humane Indian policy in the South and a national observatory.

Clay did not make a notable Secretary of State. He did not succeed in persuading Great Britain to open the West India trade to American ships or to settle the disputed boundary between Maine and Canada. Nor was he able to get Great Britain to agree to return fugitive slaves from Canada in return for an offer to return deserters from the British army and navy. William Beach Lawrence, minister to the Court of Saint James's, wrote to President Adams that Clay's instructions were too peremptory; they did not leave him enough discretion to negotiate successfully.

One of the unfortunate aspects of American diplomacy during Adams's administration was a deterioration of good relations with the Mexican Republic. Joel Poinsett, an aristocratic South Carolinian, arrived in Mexico in 1825 as the first American minister. Instead of creating good will, he stirred up antipathy to the United States. He participated in internal quarrels, especially in favoring the York rite over the Scottish rite Masons. More important, he had received instructions from Clay to buy as much of Texas as possible. The Mexicans became so hostile to Poinsett that their government asked for his recall.

Clay did secure some minor diplomatic gains. He renewed with Great Britain the treaty of joint occupation of Oregon, which expired in 1828. He concluded some commercial treaties with South American governments. He gave a new twist to the Monroe Doctrine by warning Mexico and Colombia to desist from trying to seize Cuba or Puerto Rico; if any American power should secure those islands, he declared, the United States by virtue of its geographical position was the rightful American power to absorb them.

The most significant diplomatic event during Clay's tenure of the Secretaryship of State was the American mission to the Pan-American Convention at Panama in the summer of 1826. The great liberator Simón Bolívar, who called the convention, did not invite the United States, possibly because he wished to get British support for a defensive union among the liberated Latin-American states. But Mexico and Colombia asked the United States to send delegates to the congress. Adams was unenthusiastic but yielded to Clay's persuasion. It was necessary, however, for the Senate to ratify the nominations of the two delegates and for the House of Representatives to concur in appropriating money for the mission. A heated debate occurred in both houses on the advisability of the United States' participating in this congress. The strongest objection, especially on the part of the Southerners, was the fear that slavery would be discussed and that the black republic of Haiti would be recognized. The long debate so delayed the American delegates that the Panama Congress had adjourned before they arrived (one of them died on the way). Clay attributed the opposition to the Panama mission to a factious opposition to anything advocated by Adams.

Clay's instructions to the American delegates to Panama was an able and in many respects a liberal document. He made it clear that the United States was not disposed to form any alliances with the South American republics or depart from its traditional policy of neutrality. The delegates were instructed to recommend equality of commercial privileges between the nations of the Western Hemisphere without giving to any European power special privileges and they were to endeavor to secure an adoption by the Latin-American republics of the United States' views on neutral rights, blockade, and contraband. They were not to countenance the recognition of the Negro republic of Haiti and were to warn the participants against any attempt by American republics to conquer Cuba or Puerto Rico. They were to promote religious freedom and the peaceful settlement of boundary disputes and to serve as interpreters of the republican type of government that had brought so many blessings to the United States. He suggested that the Panama conference consider the cutting of a canal across Mexico or Central America which should be open to all the ships of the world on the basis of equal tolls. Clay was very proud of these instructions, and when at the close of his life a gold medal was made for him containing a list of his achievements, he wished his authorship of the Panama instructions to be included.

Out of the debate on the Panama mission came a personal attack on Clay in the Senate by John Randolph of Roanoke that led to a famous duel. Randolph had badgered Clay on numerous occasions. In the congressional session of 1823-1824 he had made fun of Clay's lack of formal education and Clay had replied with a stinging rebuke. Now the eccentric Virginian referred to the corrupt-bargain charge, speaking of the "alliance between Old Massachusetts and Kentucky — between the frost of January, and young blythe, buxom, and blooming May — the eldest daughter of Virginia — young Kentucky — not so young, however, as not to make a prudent match and sell her charms for their full value." With satiric venom, he declared: "I was defeated, horse, foot, and dragoons — cut up — and clean broke down — by the coalition of Blifil and Black George — by the combination, unheard of till then, of the Puritan with the blackleg."

Clay had been so deeply wounded by the reiterated charge of bargain and corruption that he was keenly sensitive to criticism. His anger could not be controlled; despite the fact that Randolph was probably mentally unbalanced and that it was highly unbecoming for a cabinet officer to fight a duel, on April 1, 1826, he sent a note of challenge to his tormentor. Clay was inexpert in the handling of arms and he was theoretically opposed to dueling. Nor did he think of the happiness of his family or his duty toward them. Indeed, none of these considerations deterred him from seeking satisfaction for his wounded sense of honor.

The duel was fought on the Virginia side of the Potomac in the late evening of April 8. Randolph was in an extremely unpredictable mood; on the evening before the duel he had told General James Hamilton of South Carolina that he would not fire at Clay, for he had resolved not to make the latter's wife a widow and his children orphans. He told his second, however, that he might change his mind about shooting at Clay "if I see the devil in Clay's eye." When he appeared on the dueling field he was dressed in a peculiar manner, his slender body enveloped in a loose-fitting white flannel wrapper. At ten paces, they fired at each other and missed the mark. On the second shot Clay's bullet pierced the loose garment of the eccentric Virginian, while Randolph fired in the air. Then the two men shook hands in an outflow of chivalric emotion. Randolph jested, "You owe me a coat, Mr. Clay," and Clay replied, "I am glad the debt is no greater." Thomas Hart Benton in reviewing his long political life described it as "the last high-toned duel" that he had witnessed.

To Clay the duel brought tranquillity and peace of mind — a catharsis of the soul. Apologizing for this episode, however, he wrote, "We are strange beings!" Clay always retained an archaic sense of honor that was characteristic of the Southern gentleman. Such a feeling led him to remark a few months later concerning the tragedy of Beauchamp, the quixotic Kentuckian who avenged his wife's honor by killing her seducer, "We live in an age of romance."

V

Kentucky Planter

CLAY'S PARTICIPATION in duels tended to identify him with the Southern gentry, but even more was he attached to the Southern way of life by the acquisition of a large plantation. Ashland was the realization of a Virginia poor boy's dream, an English estate in the New World, with a two-hundred-acre woodland park that Lord Morpeth, who visited Ashland, said was the nearest approach to an English park of any he had seen in this country. Here Clay lived, with interruptions of sojourns in Washington, for over forty-five years, and here he enjoyed dispensing the hospitality of a Southern gentleman. Ashland was an almost ideal place on which to rear his large family of children. In its seclusion he planned many of his campaigns and developed his political policies, and much of his political correspondence was dated from the plantation and signed in neat, regular script, "H. Clay." His plantation, moreover, provided solace to his wounded spirit when he was defeated for the Presidency. He enjoyed immensely its flower gardens, its delicious home-grown food, and its crops growing luxuriantly in a rich soil. He was especially proud of his fine blooded stock, fattened on the lush Kentucky bluegrass. Ashland was only a mile and a half from the center of Lexington so that he and his family could easily participate in the social pleasures of a cultivated community.

This plantation of five hundred and thirteen acres Clay acquired gradually, buying the first tract in 1805 but not recording the deeds to the major portion of the estate until 1811. The imposing mansion which he built on it was probably not constructed until later. The letter books of Benjamin Latrobe in 1813 show that he made designs for the house. It was a two-and-a-half-story building, unadorned by columns, with thick brick walls, and distinguished by a three-sided vestibule having a Palladian window above it. Numerous outbuildings provided for the comforts and necessities of the mansion, a dovecote, chickenhouse, greenhouse, barns, stable, coachhouse, and, particularly interesting, two large conical-shaped icehouses which were filled in the winter and supplied ice for the master's mint juleps and the mistress's ice-cream desserts.

The furnishings of the mansion reflected Clay's tastes and achievements. There were the gold brocaded satin draperies brought from Lyons in 1815 after the Treaty of Ghent, as well as a pair of French sofas. There was the huge canopied bed in which he slept, covered with a silk quilt made by "The Ladies of Philadelphia." There were the portraits of Clay by the Kentucky artist Matthew Jouett and by G. P. A. Healy, and the marble bust by Joel T. Hart, the Kentucky sculptor. There was china brought from France in which ice cream and strawberries and rich Ashland cream were served. Clay's chess table, gold-bronze candlesticks, marble mantels, rosewood cases, chandeliers, his deerskin trunk, a portrait of Washington and his family by Inman, and cut-glass vases filled with roses marked a style of life far different from that of his poverty-stricken youth.

Associated with this luxury was a patent bedstead manufactured by Mr. Bell of Lexington, for which the great statesman wrote a testimonial. He found it "greatly superior to those in common use. . . . They will hardly ever require any precaution to destroy bugs as they afford no place of retreat to them."

As host of Ashland Clay was extremely gracious and hospitable. Numerous famous persons as well as plain American citizens visited the "Sage of Ashland." Among those who crossed the threshold were James Monroe, Aaron Burr, Martin Van Buren, William Henry Harrison, Daniel Webster, and many European visitors such as Lafayette, Harriet Martineau, and Lord Morpeth. A traveler in 1845 described a call. His nervousness over meeting the eminent statesman disappeared at once when Clay grasped his hand and by his simple, affable manner made him feel at home. "Mr. Clay sat in his easy chair, every thing about him neat and simple as his own dress, and taking his occasional pinch of snuff from a silver box, on the lid of which I could see a log cabin engraved, he looked and seemed more like the quiet happy farmer than any thing else." Clay was proud to show to visitors his garden, his green lawn and shrubs, his blooded horses and cattle, and even his Portuguese pigs.

Major-domo of the mansion was Charles, Clay's favorite slave and his valet whenever he went to Washington. Charles was the perfect servant, "a kind of second master of household to Mr. Clay, and enjoys the greatest trust and confidence. To him can the keys of the wine-cellar be given without fear and on all occasions where help was needed, Mr. C. called for Charles. Charles brought us wine, Charles was at the door, at the carriage, at the gate, every where in fact, and as polite and civil as a man asking for office. He is a fine looking middle-sized negro, about thirty years old and I do not believe he could be drawn from Mr. Clay except by absolute animal force, so great is his devotion to him."

Mrs. Clay played a dominant role in the Ashland household. Caring little for the pleasures of fashionable society, Lucretia devoted her energies to rearing eleven children and to managing the plantation during the frequent absences of the master. She gave her attention especially to the dairy and cheese-making establishments and to the garden. Some of the eggs, chickens, butter and vegetables were sold to the Phoenix Hotel in Lexington. In January, 1843, her husband wrote Lucretia from New Orleans that he had sold the hams which she had sent down the river at 12½ cents a pound and used the proceeds to buy sugar, coffee, and rice. Clay, easygoing in money matters, paid grateful tribute to Lucretia's managerial abilities and her thrift: "Again and again has she saved our home from bankruptcy." Lucretia's practical nature is illustrated by a piquant story told of her. A New England lady said to her, "Isn't it a pity that your husband gambles so much!" "Oh, I don't know," she quickly replied, "he usually wins."

A kind and hospitable woman, Mrs. Clay was a very indulgent mother who failed to discipline her boys with a steady hand. Clay himself was a lenient and tolerant father. In 1814, while he was in Europe negotiating the Treaty of Ghent, Mrs. Clay employed the New Englander Amos Kendall as a tutor for her children at a salary of $300 a year. This young graduate of Dartmouth College found that he had no easy task, for Theodore, thirteen years old, and Thomas, twelve, were almost ungovernable. Their education had been so badly neglected that they knew nothing of Latin or of English grammar.

Kendall's journal depicts a tug of war with the Clay boys. They strenuously resisted learning Latin and they were constantly fighting each other. When the tutor tried to discipline Thomas, the boy fought his schoolmaster like a tiger, cursing him and calling him "a damned Yankee rascal." In his journal the New Englander noted the evil effects of slavery on the rearing of Southern children: May 29: "Yesterday, Mrs. Clay being absent, Thomas got into a mighty rage with some of the negroes, and threatened and exerted all his little power to kill them"; August 23: "Hearing a great noise in the kitchen, I went in and found Theodore swearing in a great rage with a knife drawn in attitude to stab one of the big negroes."

Mrs. Clay, he observed, belonged to "the polite world." She was quite unlike Rachel Jackson, the wife of her husband's great rival, who liked to smoke a pipe with her husband and who spent her Sundays going to church and her Thursdays attending prayer meetings. Mrs. Clay entertained the polished aristocracy of Lexington in her drawing room, and, like the "polite world," she did not hesitate to tell small social lies to save other people's feelings. Whenever the Yankee tutor criticized the Kentuckians, she defended them in a spirited manner. Yet Kendall always retained an affection for the mistress of Ashland, who had introduced the awkward New Englander to the young ladies of Lexington and who had warmheartedly cared for him during an illness, even cooking a beefsteak for him with her own hands. In Washington, she was so kind and discreet that she never made an enemy. "She is what you call a good woman," observed Margaret Bayard Smith, "but has no qualities of mind to attract — none of the heart to endear. She is a most devoted mother, and to sew for her children is her chief, almost exclusive occupation." The deaths of many of her children seem to have made her husband more affectionate toward her as they together grew older.

Clay was a good citizen of the Lexington community. In his young manhood he promoted the Lexington library, receiving donations for its support. Although he had little formal education he was elected one of the law professors of Transylvania University, served as a trustee for many years, and took an active interest in its affairs. In 1824 he wrote to Edward Everett asking him to recommend a Harvard man for professor of mathematics for the university, "One free from objection and from peculiarity on the score of religion." In a letter to Senator Josiah Stoddert Johnston of Louisiana in 1830 asking his support for a petition of Transylvania University for a public grant of land he said, "Transylvania was the first temple of Science erected in the wilds of the West." In 1834 he tried to secure a professorship at Transylvania for the brilliant Francis Lieber, who later joined the faculty of South Carolina College and became an eminent writer on government, the author of *On Civil Liberty and Self-Government*.

In addition to his generous support of this Lexington institution, Clay rendered another service to the advancement of learning in the United States by his advocacy of an international copyright law. In 1837 he made a report to Congress in favor of such a law. After having presented the cause of American and British authors in the Senate on three occasions, he concluded that the prospect of getting Congress to enact an international copyright law was very bad. Such was his report to Francis Lieber, December 28, 1839, when he wrote that the principal opposition to the law came from the large book printers of the country, who had a powerful influence on members of Congress. This opposition could be overcome, he observed, only by enlightening public opinion, by sending petitions to Congress, numerously signed, by agitating through the press, and by sending a committee of authors to Washington to answer questions and combat objections to the proposed law before committees of Congress.

During Clay's lifetime and for many years afterwards, however, Congress refused to pass an international copyright law.

Clay's correspondence with Lieber indicates that he seldom read a book. Lieber occasionally sent him some of his books and manuscripts on political theory, which Clay acknowledged but only rapidly skimmed through. He did not have much of a library at Ashland. His speeches contained few quotations or references to books. He did, however, refer frequently to examples of Roman and Greek history, which he probably derived from reading Plutarch's *Lives* in his youth. Although he read little himself he sought to persuade his sons to become well-educated men. On December 18, 1837, he sent a list of history books for his son James to read, including Plutarch's *Lives,* Tacitus, Gillie's *Greece,* Gibbon, Hume, Russell's *Modern Europe,* Hallam's *Middle Ages,* Robertson's *Charles V,* Marshall's *Life of Washington,* and Botta's *History of the American Revolution.*

He advised his son that the great secret of happiness was constant employment. Clay himself practiced this precept of the strenuous life. Margaret Bayard Smith wrote in 1829, "Henry Clay was made for action — not for rest." Excitement was his natural medium, but he also needed the repose and tranquillity of his Kentucky plantation. To his son James he wrote at the end of his life: "For myself I believe that the chance of happiness is greater there [on the farm] than in public life."

After he retired from office as Secretary of State in 1829 he returned to Ashland to give his personal attention to the plantation. He had been active in farming only a year when he wrote his close friend Francis T. Brooke of Fredericksburg, Virginia, "My attachment to rural occupations every day acquires more strength; and if it continues to increase another year as it has the last,

I shall be fully prepared to renounce forever the strife of public life. My farm is in fine order, and my preparations for the crop of the present year are in advance of all my neighbors. I shall make a better farmer than a statesman." Nevertheless Clay could not resist the lure of public office and was a candidate for the Presidency oftener than any other man except Eugene V. Debs and Norman Thomas. Even his letter of apparent renunciation contains an account of his elation at being so cordially received during a recent visit to Louisiana and his belief that should he run for President he could count on the vote of Louisiana, whose staple, sugar, needed tariff protection as much as the hemp interest of Kentucky.

Clay employed an overseer at Ashland, and like most Southern planters he frequently changed his overseers. The Lexington newspapers contain various notices, over a period of years, in which different overseers at Ashland advertised the services of imported bulls, jacks, and stallions. When he departed for Washington Clay left detailed written instructions for the overseers which show his practical knowledge of farming. Letters from the Clay family indicate that the overseers treated the Negroes well and that some of the overseers, particularly Mr. Florea, were quite satisfactory. Others, however, were guilty of serious neglect of the plantation during the master's absences. In the fall of 1819 William Faux, an English farmer, visited Ashland and reported: "The windows are broken and the frames and doors are rotten for want of paint or tar; the gardens in a piggish state, full of weeds, the walks gullied by heavy rains; the grass borders and lawn wild, dirty, and unmowed and everything else inelegant; although the soil is rich to excess, and almost all kinds of vegetables spring spontaneously and grow luxuriantly, and the house is brimful of negroes who might keep all in the neatest order."

In December, 1833, Clay asked his son Henry Clay, Junior, to ride over from the latter's plantation, Maplewood, to report on conditions at Ashland. The younger Henry wrote that the overseer had neglected to keep up the plantation, the fences were falling down, and the slaves were not working properly. Furthermore, the overseer had been frequently absent from the plantation, being engaged in "petty trading and speculations." Clay ordered the overseer dismissed and his son Thomas Hart temporarily employed in his place, provided that the latter had "sufficiently renounced his old habits." Thomas Hart was a profligate but beloved son of Clay who had spent some time in a jail in Philadelphia.

The money crop of the Bluegrass in Clay's time was not burley tobacco, as it is today, but hemp. The slender stalks, eight to ten feet high, were cut with a knife in the middle of August and allowed to lie in the fields to be rotted by the dew so that the long fibers could be easily detached from the glutinous material of the stalk. Dew-rotted Kentucky hemp was inferior to Russian hemp rotted in vats and pools, and it was necessary to protect it from competition with foreign fibers, a fact that contributed to making Clay an advocate of a high protective tariff. Clay revealed his intimate knowledge of the art of growing hemp and preparing it for the market in a detailed letter to an agricultural society in Ohio which was published in the *Western Agriculturist and Practical Farmers Guide* of Cincinnati in October, 1830.

Most Kentucky farmers refused to go to the trouble of using the water-rotting process in preparing their hemp. They were prejudiced against the process partly because the pools and vats in which the hemp was rotted smelled bad and were believed to cause disease, but the main reason, Clay believed, was the want of water at the proper season. The master of Ashland tried the Russian method in the 1840's at Ashland and produced some superior hemp, but in the end he failed. The hardest work in preparing hemp for the market was "breaking," or separating, the fibers from the stalk. This task was done in the winter, usually by slaves, who employed a crude device known as a hemp brake. Clay was interested in the invention of a modern machine to take the place of the old device. On October 12, 1846, he wrote to Thomas L. Fortune, "I have seen so many hemp brakes tried and fail — yet I would pay $100 for your invention if successful."

Clay displayed imagination and freedom from tradition in farming and raising stock. Although he gave close attention to the experience of practical farmers, he was willing to adopt scientific innovations. He experimented with sugar beets, gave seed to his neighbors, and advocated government encouragement of the cultivation of this crop. He also tried different grasses for pasture, but he awarded top honors to bluegrass, which he believed was imported into Kentucky from England. A traveler who visited his farm in the 1840's noted that the fences were in fine order, the crops of wheat, corn, and rye were free of weeds, and that he had a ten-acre lot of corn upon which he bestowed especial care in order to win a premium at the agricultural fair.

As time passed, Clay devoted more and more of his attention and capital to stock raising. In 1831 he wrote that he was much engrossed in his farms, having purchased nearby Mansfield, containing three hundred acres. On these estates he employed fifteen hands, cultivated two hundred acres of corn, one hundred and twenty acres of other grains, and had approximately one hundred head of cattle and one hundred head of horses and mules. "There is a great difference, I think," he observed two years later, "between a farm employed in raising dead produce for market and one which is applied, as mine is, to the rearing of all kinds of livestock. I have the Maltese ass, the Arabian horse, the merino and saxe merino sheep, the English Hereford and Durham cattle, the goat, the mule, and the hog. The progress of these animals from their infancy to maturity presents a constantly varying subject of interest, and I never go out of my house without meeting with some of them to engage agreeably my attention. Then our fine green sward, our natural parks, our beautiful undulating country everywhere exhibiting combinations of grass and trees or luxuriant crops, all conspire to render home delightful."

Clay was a pioneer in importing Hereford cattle from England. He had been impressed with the Hereford red cattle when he attended the Smithfield Stock Show in 1815. After some correspondence with Peter Irving (brother of Washington Irving), who resided at Liverpool, he was able to purchase two bulls and two heifers, which were brought to Baltimore in 1817 and thence along the National Road to Ashland. Other Kentucky stock raisers followed Clay's example, but the Herefords lost their popularity and in the 1830's Durham Shorthorns displaced them as the favorite imported cattle. When Clay's famed Durham bull Orizimbo died, he announced the event to the Senate as "a great loss public and private." Clay's importations of fine English cattle improved the stock of Kentucky and his correspondence shows that in his importations of blooded stock he was motivated not merely by the hope of private profit and satisfaction, but by a desire also to be a public benefactor.

One of the most important enterprises at Ashland was the raising of mules. The mule was the common draft animal on the Southern plantations. In 1831 Clay wrote that a vast number of these animals were raised in Kentucky for the Southern market and that so great was the demand in his neighborhood for good jacks to propagate mules that he had refused $500 for one that he owned. He imported jacks and jennets from Malta, Spain, and France, seeking animals of extraordinary height. As early as 1828 his overseer advertised in the *Lexington Reporter*, "The Jackass Ulysses," imported from Malta in the naval vessel *North Carolina*, whose services would be limited for the season to thirty mares and jennets at a fee of ten dollars. Some of Clay's famous asses were the jennet Calypso and the jacks Don Manuel and Magnum Bonum; of the two latter he employed the artist Troye to paint pictures.

The Ashland plantation raised many fine specimens of mules which were driven along the roads to the Black Belt of Alabama and through the Cumberland Gap to the Southeastern plantations. One of his customers was the Whig congressman and planter Ebenezer Pettigrew, to whose plantation in eastern North Carolina he sent in 1841 twenty-three mules of high pedigree. Some of them, he informed Pettigrew, were the get of a Poitou jack brought from France, while others were produced by a Maltese jack descended from the Knight of Malta, the property of General George Washington.

Henry Clay's interest in breeding race horses was characteristic of the gentleman farmers of the Bluegrass. In 1808 the *Lexington Reporter* advertised "the Celebrated imported turf horse Buzzard" standing at stud on Clay's farm. This racing sire, imported from England, was described by one of Clay's correspondents as "the finest horse upon the Continent." In partnership with four other gentlemen Clay paid $5500 for this famous stallion. From Governor James Barbour of Virginia he purchased Allegrante, an imported brood mare for which he paid fifteen hundred dollars. When the Sultan Mahmud II gave four Arabian horses to the American minister at Constantinople in 1830, Congress confiscated them because the Constitution prohibits government officials from accepting gifts from foreign powers. Clay bought a one-half interest in one of these stallions, named Stamboul. For the purpose of training and exercising his race horses he built a private track at Ashland, one of the first private courses in Kentucky.

Clay wrote to Nicholas Biddle, the Philadelphia banker, in 1838 that he had thought it expedient to open a new source of revenue by the purchase of an English stallion. In a humorous and gossipy vein he remarked, "Our worthy little President has been represented as aspiring to the hand of the Queen Mother and his son ["Prince John"] to that of the Queen of England. If one-half of that be true, I shall be pardoned . . . for attempting to deal in far less noble and less aristocratic English blood." He would reverse, he quipped, the saying of the English monarch Richard, "I would not give my horse for a kingdom."

After his defeat as Whig candidate for President in 1844, admiring friends presented three fine thoroughbreds as gifts to him. Dr. W. N. Mercer of New Orleans sent up in the steamboat *Uncle Sam* the mare Magnolia, which he wrote had run in one race and had been "defeated but not dishonoured." This mare had thirteen foals, one of them Iroquois, a winner of the English Derby, and established such a famous bloodline that she has been described as the "Empress of the American Stud Book." The aristocratic South Carolina planter Wade Hampton II in June, 1845, sent to Clay the bay filly Margaret Wood as a token of his regard, and Commodore Morgan gave to him the stallion Yorkshire, a highly successful sire. "Long John" Wentworth in his reminiscences of Clay in 1850 relates Clay's great pride in announcing to a group at the National Hotel that one of the colts of his son John had recently won his first race, whereupon the

Kentucky statesman discoursed expertly on the descendants of English race horses imported into America.

The master of Ashland was also active in importing fine blooded sheep and pigs to improve his stock. In 1829 he purchased in Washington County, Pennsylvania, fifty full-blooded Merino sheep, which were driven on foot to Lexington. Six years later he bought eleven Saxon sheep from Hyde Park, Dutchess County, New York, which were shipped to Baltimore and from there were brought to Kentucky. Clay won prizes on both his sheep and cattle at the stock fairs in Lexington. The proximity of his farm to Lexington made it easy for dogs to kill his sheep so that finally he got rid of his pedigreed stock. In 1850 the manuscript census returns show that Ashland did not have a single sheep. He continued to raise a large number of pigs at Ashland, experimenting with the different breeds of Berkshire, China, and Portuguese. He delighted personally in feeding the pigs. Family tradition also tells that he kept a bowl of shelled corn in the dining room with which he called up his chickens.

Harriet Martineau, the English bluestocking, visited Ashland in 1835 and described the home as a very happy one. She enjoyed the flowers, trees, and birds, the sunny woods, the glades that reminded her of *Ivanhoe,* the delicious food, especially "daily piles of strawberries and mountains of ice cream," the fine horses in the stable, and "the drolleries of the little negroes." The great charm of Ashland, however, was the conversation of Mr. Clay. Miss Martineau and the Scottish traveler Charles Augustus Murray were surprised that so impetuous a person as their host could be remarkably frank, detached, and moderate in speaking of parties and personalities that were opposed to him.

Yet life at Ashland was not always the Kentucky idyll that it seemed to be to the traveler or casual visitor.

There were troubles with overseers, with runaway Negroes, with mortgages on the plantation, with numerous deaths in the family, and with the visitation of plagues. In the summer of 1833 cholera struck the Bluegrass for the first time. Nearly five hundred citizens of Lexington died, including many of Clay's friends; but fortunately the white and black family at Ashland escaped. Clay himself apparently prescribed the remedy when some of his slaves had violent abdominal pains — twenty grains of calomel, twenty grains of rhubarb, and a mixture of salt and mustard. In letters to his friend Peter B. Porter of New York he vividly described the appearance of Lexington during the plague — stores and shops closed, and no one moving in the streets except those concerned with the sick and the dead.

Clay's free and easy ways in spending money and his generosity in endorsing notes often brought him into grave financial difficulties. He was constantly borrowing and placing mortgages on his property. Among his creditors was John Jacob Astor. In 1828 his political enemies charged him with bankruptcy. Clay protested that they had searched the records of Fayette County and had "extracted from them a formidable list of mortgages which are paraded as evidences of my bankruptcy." In rebuttal, he declared that he had never been sued for an uncontested debt, that the cause of his temporary withdrawal from public life in 1821 was because of heavy financial responsibilities caused by endorsing notes for friends, but that since then he had resolved not to endorse for others except in extraordinary cases. The mortgages against his estate, he declared, were now less than ten thousand dollars and he was in good financial condition, his estate being worth approximately one hundred thousand dollars.

But on November 15, 1842, during an agricultural

depression in the South, he gave a mortgage on Ashland for $20,000 due on May 21, 1845. At least part of his mortgage was incurred in aiding his sons, particularly Thomas Hart Clay, who had failed in the hemp business. The old statesman could not meet his obligations on the due date of the mortgage, but anonymous friends raised $25,750 and paid off the mortgage so that the "Sage of Ashland" could spend his last days with a tranquil mind as to the fate of his home.

Subtly the plantation life at Ashland influenced Clay's political philosophy. Here he came into direct contact with a large number of slaves, saw slavery in its paternal aspects, and obtained an insight into race relations that no Northern statesman could have gained. Ashland was quite different from the cotton plantations. Their interests required free trade while hemp plantations like Ashland, as noted in the discussion of Clay's tariff speech of 1824, demanded protection from foreign competition. Kentucky hemp, however, was produced largely for the Southern market, its main use being for cotton bagging and plow lines. Hence a politician like Clay, who represented the hemp planters, was confronted with a painful conflict of interests. Clay responded also to the aristocratic pressures of plantation life. His manners were democratic and simple, but from his associations with the plantation gentry he tended to absorb their sense of values and conservative viewpoint. He had moved up from poverty and insignificance into the company of the Breckinridges, the Shelbys, the Combses and the Wickliffes. His stock-raising interests, moreover, brought him into the circle of the wealthy men who bred and raced blooded horses. Clay subscribed to their code of honor, their practice of lavish hospitality, and their disdain of rabble rousing.

V I

The Art of Politics
in the West

HENRY CLAY was a Bluegrass politician, the representative of a relatively conservative Western community. The "Ashland District" which sent him to Congress consisted of the counties of Fayette, Jessamine, and Woodford, the area of the best agricultural land and of the greatest concentration of slaves in the state. It was essential for the success of his presidential ambitions that he should retain the complete loyalty not only of the Bluegrass but of the entire state. Consequently, he watched the annual August elections with the keenest of interest, for they were one of the barometers of his hopes for political promotion.

Clay never won the mastery over the political life of Kentucky that Calhoun exercised in South Carolina. He was not the absolute dictator that "the Great Nullifier" became, crushing all political opposition and casting such a deep shadow over the state that young and ambitious politicians were suppressed. Yet he had tremendous prestige in Kentucky so that only once did any candidate oppose him for election to Congress. This occurred in 1816 after he had supported the passage of the unpopular Compensation Act, which raised the compensation of congressmen by substituting a salary of fifteen hundred dollars for the per-diem allowance. Numerous congressmen suffered defeat because of their unlucky votes in favor of this bill and Clay had a hard contest to keep his seat. "Gallant Harry" attacked the opposing candidate, the one-armed John Pope, as a former Federalist in a spirited debate on the hustings, and promised to work for the repeal of the controversial compensation law. Thus he managed to overcome the prejudice aroused against him among the plain people by his support of the odious measure.

His most difficult problems of local control followed the severe financial panic of 1819, producing political reverberations in Kentucky that seriously menaced Clay's leadership. As a result of popular pressure the legislature enacted a number of stay laws for the relief of debtors, created the Bank of the Commonwealth for the purpose of issuing cheap paper money, and took the great humanitarian step of abolishing the law providing for imprisonment of debtors (December 17, 1821). This latter piece of liberal legislation occurred ten years before Congress finally enacted the bill of Senator Richard M. Johnson of Kentucky abolishing imprisonment for debt in federal cases.

Clay tried to avoid becoming involved in the turmoil of the relief struggle, but his private correspondence indicates that he strongly disapproved of the acts of the relief party. He was a moderate conservative who had little sympathy with the burgeoning of a rough and tumble democracy reckless of property rights and vested interests. In the fall of 1822 he wrote to his aristocratic friend Benjamin Watkins Leigh in Virginia that although the relief party had been successful generally in the late elections, many of the seats for the legislature had been closely contested and the governor had sent a strong antirelief message to the legislature, so that "we begin to see day break."

In the following year the Court of Appeals declared

some of the relief laws unconstitutional. This overturning
of the popular will by the judiciary threw the voters
into great agitation and for approximately three years
divided the state into acrimonious factions. Clay regretted
that public opinion should have become so inflamed over
these decisions. It would have been better for the peace
of the state, he thought, if the Appellate Court could have
avoided passing on the constitutionality of the relief laws.
His statement on this point is so characteristic of the
temper of his mind, which instinctively sought to avoid
violent public controversy, that a portion of his letter is
quoted below. He did not doubt that the courts possessed
the right of declaring unconstitutional laws of the legislature invalid, but he thought the courts sometimes "pushed
the principle too far and that, erecting themselves into a
sort of tribunal to remedy . . . *all* the evils of bad legislation, they have not allowed to operate other probably
more efficacious correctives." In the end, "most of the
pernicious acts of legislation would be rectified by the operations of public sentiment. When so corrected there is
always tranquillity and general acceptance. But if, during
the existence of the excitement the Courts interpose, the
consequence is, that the public disorders are prolonged instead of being healed."

The relief party was so aroused and so powerful that its
victory in the August elections in 1824 alarmed Clay. He
feared that they would oust the appellate judges from
their office by repealing the law organizing the court.
Such a procedure he condemned as violating the constitutional security intended for the judges. But he hoped the
good sense of the legislature would reject it. These statements of Clay on the judiciary and trust in the people to
correct the evils of government are so Jeffersonian in sentiment that they could have been written by Jefferson
himself.

Clay's confidence in the wisdom of the people was unfounded, for the legislature passed on December 24, 1824, a law abolishing the old court of appeals and setting up a new court. The old court refused to abdicate, with the result that for two years there existed rival supreme courts, each claiming to be the only legal court of appeals in the state. Most of Clay's close friends supported the "Old Court." One of these, John J. Crittenden, wrote to Clay in 1825 that a state of anarchy existed in Kentucky and that he had postponed introducing resolutions in the legislature endorsing Clay and Adams because of fear that the relief party would defeat them. Nearly a year later he commented that Kentucky politics were based on feeling and resembled a mighty quicksand. But on December 30, 1826, the legislature abolished the New Court and the conservatives reasserted their dominance over the state government. Bitter feelings, however, continued for years to exist between the former Old Court and New Court factions.

Clay pursued a conscious policy of avoiding active intervention in local politics. He kept himself informed on state affairs by letters from his friends and relatives. In 1830 Crittenden appealed to Clay to intervene in state elections to get the proper men to run as candidates for the legislature. But in making this request he apologized, "I know that you have almost a fastidious disinclination to interfere in such subjects." Clay's policy of abstaining from obvious participation in state politics arose partly from an Olympian conception of the role of the national statesman. Also there was less reason for him to interfere in state politics since he did not have to struggle to retain his seat in Congress.

Clay's prestige as a national political leader, however, was at stake in the presidential election of 1828, when Adams was a candidate for re-election. The partisans of General Jackson made vigorous preparations to elect "the hero of New Orleans," who, they maintained, had been cheated out of the office by a corrupt bargain between Clay and Adams. In Congress they formed a vociferous party that, largely for political effect, attacked practically every measure and policy of the Adams administration. The President, remarkably aloof from the game of playing politics, refused to use the patronage to strengthen his position, declining to remove from the federal service even those who were actively hostile to him. Although the Secretary of State was not a spoilsman, he believed in pursuing a moderate course in regard to appointments and removals from office. Accordingly, he advocated the dismissal from the federal service of those who actively opposed the executive policies.

Clay, despite ill health, virtually took charge of Adams's campaign for re-election. In Kentucky he realized that he would have a hard fight to keep the state from going over to Jackson. The struggle over the relief laws and the Old and New Court issue had stirred the voters profoundly and had brought to the surface the radical elements and the smoldering discontent of the common people. The supporters of the New Court largely went into the Jacksonian movement. Among Clay's former friends who joined the opposition party were Colonel Richard M. Johnson, one of the most popular men of the state; Francis P. Blair and Amos Kendall — the former tutor of the Clay boys — both Kentucky editors to become powerful in the Kitchen Cabinet; and William T. Barry, Chief Justice of the New Court, whom Jackson appointed Attorney General.

Realizing the progress that the Jacksonians were making in Kentucky, Clay bestirred himself to counteract their efforts. In 1827 he wrote to his lieutenants from Washington urging a thorough organization of the Clay and

Adams forces. He proposed that an elaborate system of committees should be established to win public support. These committees, he suggested, should call public meetings in every county to support Adams and should collect campaign literature to distribute among the voters. He urged that these public meetings pass resolutions approving of Adams's administration and "particularly resolutions expressive of their detestation of the calumny by which their fellow-citizen [Clay] has been assailed; of their confidence in him and of their conviction of the entire failure to establish through Mr. Buchanan anything injurious to his character." In the August elections of 1828, nevertheless, the Jackson party won control of the legislature and elected the lieutenant governor, but its candidate for governor, William T. Barry, was defeated by a narrow margin.

The Jacksonians also triumphantly carried the presidential election of that year. Even those Western states which in 1824 had voted for "Harry of the West," Kentucky, Ohio, and Missouri, deserted him to vote for "the Old Hero." Two weeks after the election Clay wrote to a correspondent, "Nothing has ever heretofore occurred to create in my mind such awful apprehensions of the permanency of our liberty."

The election of 1828 sharply revealed that the day of the old type of politician was over and that new men and a new type of politics had arrived. While James Monroe, the last of "the Virginia dynasty," was President, there still lingered the tradition of the early Republic, that a gentleman should not seek public office but that the office should seek him. The electorate was relatively small, for many of the common people did not have the vote. Moreover, the common people regarded governmental officials with respect as men whose personal opinions had great weight. The leading figures in public affairs were not forced as a rule to truckle to popular passions and whims. The best of them were philosopher-statesmen, well grounded in a knowledge of political theory, of Locke, Sidney, Harrington, and the debates of the Constitutional Convention of 1787.

Yet in Clay's lifetime, a revolution took place in the political mores of the American people. The aristocratic attitude toward politics disappeared with the spread of Jacksonian democracy. The politician then tried to identify himself with the common people, to wear old clothes, claim a log-cabin origin, and conceal his superior education and his command of the king's English. It became a common practice to treat the voters with whiskey and to speak grandiloquently of "the sovereign people." Kemp Battle, who was long the president of the University of North Carolina, described this custom in his *Memories of an Old-Time Tar Heel*. He witnessed a candidate for office in a mountain village in North Carolina who harangued the Demos, standing before a grog shop waving in his hand a tin quart pot to give point to his arguments. After his speech was finished he invited the sovereign people to follow him into the shop. He was elected.

Clay, however, retained something of the old dignity in political campaigns. He was very anxious to give the impression that he did not seek public office. He tried to conduct himself in his campaigns as a statesman of the old Virginia school. When he was invited to visit the commencement exercises of Franklin College at Athens, Georgia, in 1838, he declined, explaining that his attendance would be construed as political in intent. "My duty," he wrote, "is to remain perfectly passive and suffer the public judgment to be formed unaffected by personal efforts of my own." The Presidency, he declared, was neither to be sought nor declined. As for himself, he would use "means to attain it only reconcilable to the nicest sense of honor and the strictest propriety."

The crude democracy of Jackson's time, moreover, led to a lower quality of government. The voters, de Tocqueville observed, failed to elect their superior men to office. To obtain the suffrage of the people it was not necessary for a politician to have a superior education or a brilliant mind. Rather, he must be able to sense the common man's discontents, his economic grievances, his prejudices, and his dreams. The successful politician in the 1830's and 1840's was, as a rule, a vigorous or eloquent stump speaker, a man who could devise popular slogans and organize political workers, and who gave the common people a feeling of their own importance. As party warfare developed into violent partisanship and as sectional tensions arose, the politician who had strong convictions and had taken a courageous public stand on issues was often pushed aside in favor of a candidate of availability. This development operated as an important factor in preventing Henry Clay from ever becoming President.

Clay was well aware of the fact that elections were more often won by good organization and by emotional appeals to the voters than by intelligent issues. When he was a candidate for the Presidency in 1832 the Jacksonians in Kentucky elected their candidate for governor in the August elections. He wrote to a correspondent that he was mortified by this defeat, which he attributed to Tennessee voters crossing the state line into the border counties and illegally voting and also to the circumstance that the Whig candidate for governor was a Presbyterian and "against that sect the most deep rooted and inveterate prejudices exist" in the state, so that he estimated the Whigs lost not less than three thousand votes.

Clay recognized the value of appealing to the voters by means of eloquent speeches, barbecues, Clay clubs, Clay balls, by thorough organization in the states, by distribution of campaign literature, and by campaign biographies. With toasts at banquets he presented slogans for his party. He was accused of writing anonymously and of inspiring editorials and articles for the newspapers. In Kentucky his chief political organs were the Lexington *Observer and Reporter,* the Louisville *Journal,* and the Frankfort *Commonwealth,* while nationally he was supported by the influential *National Intelligencer* of Washington and Hezekiah Niles's *Niles' Weekly Register* of Baltimore.

The Kentucky politician often expressed a fear that his opponent would influence elections by the corrupt use of money. His own attitude toward money and politics was more ethical than that of his rival Webster, but perhaps not as admirable as that of the high-minded Calhoun. His personal borrowing from the Bank of the United States may have had some bearing on his political activity. In 1827 Clay requested Webster to collect money from the Eastern cities to subsidize the anti-Jackson newspapers of Hammond at Cincinnati and Pleasants in Richmond. The Massachusetts politician responded by collecting the desired funds. Although Clay did not have the enslaving love of money that Webster exhibited, nevertheless he sought the friendship of the same men, the Northern industrialists, who patronized Webster, because he wanted their votes.

Clay's ideals of political behavior belonged to the early Republic, when leaders like Jefferson, Madison, and Monroe scorned demagoguery. In 1827, when the party of Jackson won alarming victories in the congressional elections in Kentucky, Clay refused to resort to some of their low tactics, admonishing his supporters not to employ "means of detraction and corruption, which we would scorn to use, and with which we would not sully our cause." Only honorable and legitimate methods to win the voters should be used. Furthermore, he consistently declared in private letters that he would make no political deals or bargains, but if elected would enter office untrammeled and free of commitments.

In the election of 1840, when William Henry Harrison was the Whig candidate for President and the Whigs engaged in an undignified campaign featuring log cabins, hard cider, and coonskins, Clay was faced by a dilemma. He regretted the practice "of appealing to the feelings and passions of our Countrymen, rather than to their reasons and judgments to secure his election. The best and only justification of this course is to be found in the practise, which was resorted to in the instance of the election of General Jackson. But that does not prevent my regret that either party should have ever been induced to employ such means." He was also very much disturbed that the Whig party failed to adopt a platform for the campaign of 1840. He believed that both parties and candidates should appeal to the voters on the basis of principles. In a confidential letter to John M. Clayton in May of that year he wrote that he was thinking of promulgating a "creed" for the Whig party, for he feared that the Democrats would say that the Whigs had no principles which they dared openly to avow. He hesitated, however, to carry out his plan, for "The danger is of supplying fresh aliment for demagogues." He finally decided not to promulgate his proposed platform for the party.

One of the attributes which Clay thought was essential for the public officer was consistency. He upheld the necessity for consistency in order to maintain the confidence of the people in the judgment and sincerity of a politician. In a speech at Lexington in 1842 reviewing his political career he declared that the only inconsistency which marred his record was the reversal of his position on a national bank. Actually, after the great change following the Treaty of Ghent, Clay's career was far more consistent than the records of the major politicians of the period.

Clay's use of the patronage in advancing his political interests is commendable in comparison with the practices of his opponents. It is true that when he was Secretary of State under Adams he tried to persuade that stern Puritan to use the patronage to strengthen his administration. But Adams refused to make realistic concessions to political expediency and lost the election of 1828. Clay's party was out of power from 1829 to 1841, when Harrison was inaugurated. After the election Clay had an interview with Harrison in Lexington and made some suggestions as to cabinet appointments, especially the necessity of having Webster in the cabinet, but Harrison was noncommittal on cabinet appointments. In the following February Clay wrote to his intimate friend Peter B. Porter in New York that he had adopted the rule of noninterference in official appointments except on rare occasions in order to prevent very bad selections. To another friend he declared that he had not recommended a person for any position in the federal government for a period of twelve years. The victory of the Whigs in 1840 brought no patronage to the great Whig leader. In a letter to President Harrison of March 15 he said that "A thousand times have my feelings been wounded" in replying to office seekers that he was "obliged to abstain from interference in all appointments."

When the Whigs were victorious in 1848, Clay wrote to the President asking for the appointment of his son James Brown Clay to a diplomatic post. He said that he had never during the course of his life used his political influence to secure the appointment of a relative. He was departing from his rule in seeking the appointment of his **son to a** diplomatic mission. He described his son as thirty-two years old, free from dissipation, industrious, and an able lawyer. Taylor appointed James to the post at Lisbon.

The death of Taylor in the summer of 1850 placed Millard Fillmore, a friend of Clay's, in power. Shortly afterwards Clay wrote the new President that he made no demands as to the patronage in Kentucky, but that he hoped his son would be retained in charge of the Portuguese mission. He also made some suggestions as to the appointments of Whigs outside of Kentucky. Surveying the appointments in the different states, he observed that Georgia, whose congressmen had been "far from supporting your administration," had received more patronage than any other state. He protested against the appointment of Henry Hilliard of Alabama, who had opposed Whig measures as regards the tariff, the organization of the House of Representatives, and the River and Harbor bill. "To see foes promoted and friends, overlooked," he warned, "has a discouraging effect. Should you not exercise more control in the patronage of the several Departments? An intimation of your wish to any of them ought to be decisive."

Clay was not an original political thinker and he did not make any notable contribution to political theory, as did Calhoun. Clay had a more optimistic view of human nature than that which the stern Calvinistic senator from South Carolina expressed in his political writings. When his friend Francis Brooke wrote to him on November 3, 1838, that the Bluegrass politician entertained too high a view of human nature he replied, "I confess that I have throughout life striven to think well of them [people], but the last thirteen years have shaken my faith very much. I yet, however, believe the mass to be honest, although very liable to deception." Clay had much reason to lower his opinion of human nature, for as he told Alexander H. H. Stuart when the latter visited Ashland in 1839, he had been the subject of more obloquy than any man living. He consoled himself by observing that such abuse was the price that every man who becomes prominent in public affairs must pay. Washington, Jefferson, and Madison, he pointed out, were represented in their day and generation as being among the vilest of the vile.

Clay was a Madisonian in political theory. On one occasion he said that Madison was the greatest statesman whom the United States had produced, with the exception of Washington. Although he believed that Jefferson had more genius than the younger statesman, he thought that at the same time he was visionary and lacking the common sense which was characteristic of Madison. In 1831 he wrote that his constitutional doctrines were those of the epoch of 1798. "I am against all power not delegated, or not necessary and proper to execute what is delegated," he wrote. "I am against all nullification, all new lights in politics, if not in religion. . . . Applying the very principles of Mr. Madison's famous interpretation of the Constitution, in the Virginia address, I find in the Constitution the power to protect our industry, and to improve our country by objects of a national character."

He was thus a moderate conservative in his political views. His conservatism was based on his belief that change in society should be accomplished by political means in a gradual fashion so that all interests would be protected. This point of view was best expressed in a letter to Francis Lieber of January 18, 1838, praising the latter's *Political Hermeneutics,* particularly the section on "Precedents." The legislature of a free country was obligated, he wrote, "to conform to those expositions of its constitution, which may have been often and deliberately made. If considerations of security and stability to private rights require that judicial precedents should not be lightly departed from, the same considerations of stability and security in respect to the rights of the whole nation enjoin that fundamental principles, which have been deliberately settled in the administration of the government should not be too easily departed from."

Clay's conservatism was not expressed in a desire to curb political democracy. He encouraged a practice of expressing the popular will in memorials to Congress and by putting pressure on congressmen by the writing of letters to them. He believed also in the exercise of the right of legislative instruction of the senators, despite the fact that it was used as a weapon by the Jacksonians against his party. Although a majority of the congressmen from the slave states were opposed to the abolitionists' exercising their constitutional right of freedom of petition, he upheld that right.

Circumstance rather than reasoned conviction, probably, led him to become a strong champion of the prerogative of the Senate against the power of the President. The expansion of the executive powers during Jackson's administrations, he thought, distorted the Constitution. "The election of Gen. Jackson," he wrote to an English traveler, "ought to be regarded as an exception from the general good sense with which the American people have conducted their affairs." Jackson's vetoes he regarded with extreme aversion and disgust. He therefore strongly favored limiting the veto power of the President as well as amending the Constitution to limit the President to a single term.

"Harry of the West" was a strong nationalist, but, like Madison, he believed firmly in preserving a proper balance between the federal and state power. His belief in a truly federal government underlay his strong opposition to any interference with slavery within the states by the federal government. Its powers were strictly limited to national affairs, he maintained, and did not extend to the domestic institutions or the police powers of the state.

Henry Clay was a skilled practitioner in the art of politics as that art was developed within the conditions of the United States of the 1830's and 1840's. His first rule was the principle of empiricism. "It is a rule with me, when acting either in a public or a private character," he wrote, "to attempt nothing more than what there exists a prospect of accomplishment." He thought that he acted from fixed political principles, but actually he moved largely by intuition, playing by ear, very much as another master politician of the era, Andrew Jackson, did. Jackson called Clay "that Demogogue," but "Harry of the West" thought that Jackson was the crafty demagogue who under the mask of being an exponent of democracy was destroying "pure republican government." Actually, neither was a demagogue in the ordinary connotation of that term; both were practicing a new type of politics that was conditioned by the rise of the common man into political power in America.

The true story of politics in America is often to be found not in the formal actions of politicians, but in their informal contacts with each other. In the boardinghouses of Washington, in the congressional "messes," at the whist table, and in the committee rooms congressmen initiated bills and made deals and formed alliances that determined the course of legislation. Clay was undoubtedly highly effective in these informal and mostly unrecorded contacts. An example of his skill in practical politics, revealing his native shrewdness, occurred in 1833, when he suppressed a rebellion in the ranks of the anti-Jackson coalition. Webster temporarily deserted his allies during and immediately after the nullification crisis by joining Jackson and seeking to form a new nationalistic party on the basis of the preservation of the Union. Clay won him back to his old allegiance by cleverly securing his selection as chairman of the strategic Senate Committee on Finance, where he would be forced to oppose Jackson's bank policy. Clay was a practical politician in the sense that a statesman must use the art of politics to accomplish desirable social and political reforms.

Abraham Lincoln called Henry Clay "my beau ideal of a statesman, the man for whom I fought all my humble life." Dennis Hanks, his cousin, in attempting to account for the fact that Lincoln became a Whig when his family and relations were Jacksonians, said he "always Loved Hen Clays Speaches I think was the Cause Mostly." Lincoln campaigned for the election of Clay as President, ardently supporting his platform of the American System. Yet the Illinois politician described the methods of Clay in terms that do not befit the beau ideal of a statesman. When Clay wished to carry an important measure, he took care that its language was not offensive to those whose support was indispensable. "He then presented it to the strong men whose help he must have or whose opposition he must stifle, and who were of strong wills, and either argued them into support or made modifications as they insisted on, or added palatable features to suit them, and thus got a powerful force enlisted in behalf of his measure; — then he visited the members of feeble wills and simply bullied them into its support without yielding one iota to them."

Clay was particularly effective in the party caucus, a relatively new device for determining party strategy. William Gilmore Simms, the Southern novelist, in a letter to Senator James H. Hammond in 1858 described such a caucus held by the Whigs during Harrison's brief administration. Simms's account belongs to the realm of oral history, for it was based on a description given him probably by a South Carolina congressman. The question before the caucus was whether to recommend to the President the summoning of an extra session of Congress, a proposal strongly favored by Clay. At this caucus, according to Simms, all the members except two were opposed to the calling of an extra session. But Clay "entered the assembly, passed down its lines, speaking as he went, in triumphant manner, with bold fearless eloquence, breast open, and, at length, confronting Webster, he seemed to concentrate the whole weight of what he had to say upon him. And so powerful was his eloquence, so keen his shafts, so personal their aim, that Webster actually crouched under him, and slid down in his seat, so that his head was almost on a level with his belly. And Clay triumphed. There were but *two* after he was done, who voted in opposition to the measure."

Yet Clay had one serious defect that disqualified him from being a consummate master of the political art: he talked too much and wrote too many letters. His devoted follower, Congressman Robert Letcher, who indiscriminately referred to the great man as "the old Prince" or "the old horse," realized this defect and tried to restrain him. Clay's friends were afraid that he would express himself too freely during the preconvention campaign of 1844. Accordingly, Letcher wrote to Crittenden: "The old Prince must hereafter remain a little quiet and *hold his jaw*. In fact he must be *caged* — thats the point — *cage him*. But he swears by all the Gods, he will keep cool and stay at home. I rather think he will be entirely prudent, tho' I have some occasional fears that he may write too many letters." It was impossible, however, for Clay to be a sphinxlike politician or to follow the noncommittal course that later brought success to Calvin Coolidge, who won the sobriquet of "Silent Cal."

A comparison of Clay with his rival Andrew Jackson reveals another deficiency of the Kentuckian as a politician. American politics has demonstrated again and again that the surest way for a politician to win votes is by identifying himself with the average man through folksiness, especially by shaking hands, remembering the first names of plain citizens, and by a warm sincerity of manner. These are more important than orations or platforms. Clay was affable and simple in manner, but his success and associations had made him a dignified gentleman rather removed from the level of thought of the common people. Jackson was closer to them because he was earthier and more coarse-grained and shared their prejudices. He was a man whom they could trust, a good hater and a violent denouncer. Although Clay had numerous friends they were not the little people. In his speeches and letters he does not say much about the working man; his main concern was for the manufacturer and the wealthy planter.

V I I

Leader of the Opposition.

At the close of February, 1829, Clay began to make preparations to leave his post as Secretary of State in the Adams administration. He sold the furniture of his home in Washington at auction and on March 15 he and his family left the capital for Ashland. His journey homeward revealed his great personal popularity. He had "never experienced more testimonies of respect and confidence, nor more enthusiasm. Dinners, suppers, balls, etc." He had "literally a free passage." Taverns, stages, and toll-gates were opened to him free from all charge. "Monarchs might be proud of the reception" he found everywhere. This was heady wine to Clay, who even then was planning to become a candidate for the Presidency in 1832.

He had hardly been comfortably settled at Ashland when he fired one of his big guns in the campaign to overthrow Jackson. On May 16 at a public dinner in Lexington he denounced the President for his flagrant exploitation of the spoils system and his appointment of congressmen to federal office. Jackson's veto of the Maysville Turnpike bill in 1830 also strengthened the Clay forces in Kentucky and the Ohio Valley. Clay misjudged the situation in thinking that the veto had caused the defection of any considerable number of Jackson men in the state and that it sealed the fate of Jackson in all the West.

The veto gave the opposition, Clay thought, an opportunity to strike a crippling blow at the administration. This could be done, he suggested, by introducing a constitutional amendment in Congress permitting bills that were vetoed by the President to be passed by a simple majority instead of a two-thirds majority of the vote of Congress. Such a maneuver, he believed, would lead to a defense of the two-thirds majority rule by the Jacksonians, and then, he gleefully observed, "We shall get the weather gage of them" and "put them on the aristocratic bench." He also urged his friend Adam Beatty at Maysville to get up public meetings for the purpose of passing resolutions condemning Jackson's policies.

The August, 1831, elections in Kentucky were watched by politicians throughout the country as an indicator of the relative strength of Clay and Jackson. Although Clay's party, the National Republicans, won control of the legislature, thus insuring the election of a National Republican senator, the Jacksonians, or Democratic Republicans, were able to elect eight of the twelve congressmen of the Kentucky delegation. This disappointing showing led to a "Clay for Senator" movement. John J. Crittenden renounced his claims to permit the legislature to send Kentucky's "favorite son" to the Senate. Clay took his seat in that body in December, 1831, and in the same month the National Republican party, meeting in convention in Baltimore, unanimously nominated him for President.

Clay's platform was essentially conservative, more appealing to the Northeast than to the West. He advocated the renewal of the charter of the United States Bank, the preservation of the protective principle in the federal tariff, and the distribution of the proceeds from the sale of the public lands to the states. Such a program could not be expected to win the approval of Southern states other than Louisiana, but it was a natural outgrowth of his economic views.

Clay hoped to win the vote of the West, but his public land policy was far from representing the views of the New West. Kentucky had no public lands in her borders and therefore her interest in the public domain was quite similar to the attitude of the Eastern states. Clay proposed to use the public lands as a source of revenue for the states to finance internal improvements. He therefore voted against schemes for giving the public lands to the states in which they lay, or Benton's graduation scheme, which would have lowered the price of federal lands, or pre-emption proposals. Indirectly his land policy would have retarded the westward movement of population and would have tended to conserve the Eastern labor market.

The issue became clear in March, 1832, when Clay presented his distribution bill to the Senate. This bill provided that the Western states should receive fifteen per cent of the proceeds from the sale of public lands lying within their borders, while the remainder should be distributed to all the states in accordance with their representation in Congress, to be used for internal improvements, education, the colonization of free Negroes, and the reduction of state debts. By opposing the cession of the public domain to the Western states or any important reduction of price of these lands he appealed to the East; and by providing a fund for internal improvements he hoped to mollify the West. But Westerners desired cheap or free lands more ardently than they wished internal improvements. His bill passed the Senate, but opposition in the House of Representatives delayed a vote until the next session of Congress.

More important in the presidential campaign of 1832

was the question of the recharter of the Second Bank of the United States. Although the charter was not due to expire until 1836, Jackson had already declared his opposition to its renewal. It was imperative, therefore, that the bank apply for a recharter when political conditions were such that the President would be likely to withhold a veto. In the fall of 1830 Clay had advised Nicholas Biddle, president of the bank, not to apply for a recharter until after the election of 1832. A year later, however, he changed his mind and urged Biddle to apply immediately, predicting that Jackson would not then negative the recharter, but might do so if the bank waited until after he was elected.

Biddle was very reluctant to follow this advice, for he feared it would make the bank a football of politics. He sent his agents, therefore, to Washington to ascertain the opinion of Congress and of prominent friends of the great financial institution. Webster, who was on the payroll of the bank, emphatically advised the bank president to apply for a new charter without delay. Biddle and his agents realized that both Clay and Webster were guided by party considerations. Nevertheless, Biddle made the decision early in January, 1832, to memorialize Congress for a new charter, apparently strongly influenced by the advice of George McDuffie of South Carolina, who presented the memorial in the House of Representatives. No doubt too his imperious and patrician nature resented the necessity for truckling to the whims of a crude upstart like Jackson, who happened to be President.

Clay, Webster, and the National Republican politicians underestimated the popular prejudice against the bank. They believed that if Jackson dared to veto a recharter bill the issue would make excellent capital in the approaching presidential election. The bill passed Congress as they expected, but Jackson on July 10 vetoed it in a message that was a masterpiece of appeal to the demo-cratic instincts of the people. He placed his opposition to the recharter on the need to strike down a great financial monopoly that corrupted the press and national politics, making the rich richer and the poor poorer. Biddle was delighted with the message; it had "all the fury of a chained panther biting the bar of his cage. It is really a manifesto of anarchy . . ." Clay denounced it in the Sen-ate and it became the paramount issue of the presidential campaign of 1832.

The National Republicans endeavored to make the tariff also an important issue of the campaign. This was Clay's pet project, which was threatened by a dangerous antitariff movement in South Carolina. His speech in New Orleans in February, 1831, was a good example of his arguments for retaining tariff protection. He pointed out that the protected sugar industry provided a home market for many products outside of the sugar region, that the profit made by the sugar planters was moderate, only five or six per cent, and that the destruction of the sugar growers by lowering the tariff would lead only to a diver-sion of labor to cotton, which was already overproduced.

In this presidential election year Clay proposed to make the protective policy more palatable by revising the Tariff of Abominations. On December 28, 1831, he presided over a meeting of the opposition members of Congress to devise a tariff measure that would give the maximum of protec-tion with the minimum of revenue. He proposed the im-mediate and total repeal of duties on noncompetitive arti-cles such as tea, coffee, spices, and wines but at the same time raising the duties on commodities that competed with American industries so as to make their importation practically prohibitive. Clay's manner of conducting the meeting, according to J. Q. Adams's diary, despite "many courtesies of personal politeness" was "exceedingly peremptory and dogmatical." When Adams, chairman of the strategic House Committee on Manufactures, objected that Clay's plan would be a defiance of the South as well as of President Jackson, who was anxious to pay the national debt before March 4, 1833, "Mr. Clay," the diary relates, "said he did not care who it defied. To preserve, maintain, and strengthen the American system he would defy the South, the President, and the devil." The Tariff Act of 1832 carried out substantially his desires, but it was the immediate cause of the nullification movement.

An unpredictable element entered the campaign with the rise of the Anti-Masonic party, which had nominated William Wirt as its candidate for President. Clay had at one time been a member of the Masonic order but not "a bright Mason," and he had withdrawn his membership some years before. His policy toward the new party was one of neutrality, although in private letters he expressed his belief that anti-Masonry should not be an issue in politics. The Anti-Masons, however, tried to force from him a public expression of opinion on the main plank of their platform, which advocated the outlawing of all secret fraternal organizations. In reply, Clay declared that he would not be "a party in the contest over masonry." The Constitution did not give the President the power to deal with the subject, and therefore the question should not enter a presidential campaign. However, he urged his supporters not to attack the Anti-Masons but to pursue a conciliatory course. He was optimistic that eventually its members would vote for him.

Although Clay himself refused to electioneer obviously, at the same time he stimulated his lieutenants to renewed exertions. His campaign manager, Senator Josiah Johnston of Louisiana, distributed speeches and pamphlets. Also Clay sought to animate the party's adherents in Virginia, his native state, which he believed could be reclaimed from Jacksonianism by proper exertion. Accordingly he wrote to Judge Brooke urging that the counties be divided into sections with workers assigned to each section to convert the voters and that vigilance committees be established to bring the voters to the polls on election day.

Clay carried the banner of an unpopular cause in the election of 1832 and he went down to defeat. His opponent had the advantage of being a military hero and of being able to dramatize himself as the representative of the rising democratic sentiment of the country. Being free of antislavery sentiment and not prominently identified with the tariff, he was more acceptable to the South than was the Kentuckian. Clay won the votes of Kentucky, Maryland, Delaware, Massachusetts, Rhode Island, and Connecticut, but he did not carry a single state of the lower South or of the New West. His electoral vote was only forty-nine as compared to the two hundred and nineteen votes received by Jackson. His friends attributed this disastrous defeat, at least in part, to the diversion of the Anti-Masonic party. The real reason, however, was the belief of the masses that Jackson was fighting for their interests against a moneyed aristocracy.

Although defeated as a presidential candidate, Clay remained, next to the President, the most powerful man in the federal government. He was leader of the opposition in a period when a strong and aggressive new party was forming. Party politics in the United States had fallen into a quiescent state during the one-party period of Monroe's administrations. This stagnant condition had begun to change in the presidential campaign of 1824 and by the time of Jackson's second administration had reached one of the high points in the history of American partisanship. Two great divisive movements, the struggle between business and democracy and the growth of sectionalism, underlay the party warfare of this period. Mingled in these conflicts and enhancing their bitterness were the clashing ambitions of some of the most outstanding personalities which American politics has produced. The rivalries among Clay, Jackson, Calhoun, and Webster represented deep economic and social forces.

The first severe strain on the bonds of Union since the struggle over the admission of Missouri occurred as a result of the rapid rise of one section of the country and the relative decline of another. South Carolina in common with the older parts of the South suffered an economic decline in the 1820's and 1830's, which she attributed largely to the unfair subsidy by the tariff of the manufacturing interests of the Northeast to the detriment of the agricultural interest. Although the high tariff policy did affect the planter adversely, the main cause of this distress was the competition of the virgin soils of the rapidly opening Southwest with the worn-out and eroded soils of the South Atlantic area. Her leaders turned, nonetheless, to political means for a remedy, to the device of nullification, or "state veto," of the obnoxious federal laws. The nullification movement was a conflict between the sovereignty of the nation and economic and political federalism.

In this controversy Clay, representing the Western point of view, supported the national idea. His freedom from sectionalism was displayed in a letter that he wrote to a Baltimore editor recalling a visit to the New England states in 1818 to see his son, a student at Harvard College. He had been "astonished at the unjust prejudices prevailing at the South against them and I returned full of admiration and esteem for them and of gratitude too for their kind and hospitable treatment of me." He was convinced there was "not a better, more moral and religious, or more enterprizing and industrious people upon earth than the descendants of the pilgrims." With this attitude to the North, he naturally wished to compromise disturbing sectional conflicts. Moreover, as a follower of Madison in his interpretation of the Constitution, he did not believe that Calhoun's doctrine of nullification had any justification in Constitutional theory.

The nullification controversy reached an alarming crisis when on November 24, 1832, a South Carolina convention declared the Tariff Acts of 1828 and 1832 null and void. Jackson was as strong a nationalist as Clay but his method of combating nullification was by the direct action of the soldier instead of the art of compromise and conciliation. His proclamation of December 10 was a stern warning against violating the laws of the United States; any attempt to break up the Union, he declared, would be treason. Clay thought the proclamation too strongly biased on the side of consolidation, or, as he expressed it, some parts were "entirely too ultra for me, and which I cannot stomach." He thought too that Jackson had encouraged the state rights intransigence of South Carolina by earlier allowing Georgia to disobey a ruling of the Supreme Court in the Cherokee Indian controversy.

In this excited situation, which threatened a clash of arms between South Carolina and the President, various measures were proposed in Congress to remove the cause of conflict. Clay was alarmed for the safety of the American system by the introduction of the Verplanck bill (December 27), which proposed to reduce the tariff approximately fifty per cent by the end of 1834. In the middle of January, 1833, he commented in a letter to a friend that he had been meditating on a plan for the settlement of the controversy but since both parties had treated him badly he was tempted to let them fight it out without intervening. Any plan that he proposed would, he observed, be instantly opposed simply because of his authorship. The controversy, he believed, was deeply intertwined with the presidential ambitions of Van Buren and Calhoun.

Nevertheless, Clay instinctively acted to take the lead in the crisis. He believed that South Carolina would not stand alone if Jackson should attempt to use force against her, but that other Southern states would join her. This fear motivated him in bringing forward his compromise tariff bill. Introduced on February 12, this bill provided for the gradual lowering of the tariff until by July 1, 1842, the duties would be only twenty per cent ad valorem. The high tariff forces succeeded in adding an amendment specifying the home evaluation of imported goods.

The manufacturers of the Northeast and high tariff advocates in general were at first opposed to the Compromise Tariff Act and Clay was accused of sacrificing his American system. Actually, he regarded his bill as bending before the storm and saving the protective system from more drastic measures which threatened a total sacrifice of the American system. His own bill would "protect the manufacturers for the present and gain time, with its chapter of accidents for them," and "preserve the Union, prevent civil war, and save us the danger of entrusting to Jackson large armies."

Clay alone, Van Buren thought, had the power to prevent a clash between South Carolina and the President. Webster favored an obstinate stand; Clay too could have folded his arms and refused to intervene. But he chose to pursue the course of conciliation, out of motives both of patriotism and personal advantage. His Compromise Tariff passed both houses of Congress, Calhoun voting for it, and became a law shortly before Congress adjourned in March, 1833. On the same day that the President signed the Compromise Tariff bill, he also signed the Force bill, which gave him extensive powers to suppress nullification. Clay seems to have approved of the Force bill as a last resort, but he was not present when the Senate passed it with only one dissenting vote, that of John Tyler.

On March 2, Clay commented, "Yesterday was perhaps the most important Congressional day that ever occurred," for on that day Congress passed the Compromise Tariff bill, the Force bill, and Clay's bill for distributing the proceeds from land sales to the states. He had the further satisfaction of receiving a letter from Abbott Lawrence, the powerful New England industrialist, stating that Clay's prestige in that section had been increased by the passage of his compromise adjustment. Indeed, these events greatly increased Clay's popularity. He had definitely won a victory over his rival Webster, who had joined the President during the nullification controversy. Hereafter Clay was often referred to as the "Great Pacificator."

In the meanwhile Jackson had begun a bold policy of removing the government deposits from the Second Bank of the United States. Despite the fact that an investigation of the bank had proved it to be in sound condition, and despite the fact that the House of Representatives had by an overwhelming vote resolved that the government deposits were safe, Jackson had concluded that as long as the deposits were controlled by the will of one man, Nicholas Biddle, they were not safe. The bank was a "hydra of corruption" that subsidized the press and used its wealth to influence elections. When two of his Secretaries of the Treasury opposed his drastic policy of depriving the bank of the government deposits, he read a paper to his cabinet on September 18 stating his intention to have the deposits removed and assuming responsibility for carrying out this policy. After dismissing Secre-

tary of the Treasury William J. Duane, he appointed
Roger B. Taney, who issued the desired order, to the
great outrage of conservative men of the country.

When Clay returned to the Senate in December he
took charge of the bank's adherents in Congress. Nicholas
Biddle selected Clay over Webster to conduct the fight to
force the President to order the return of the deposits.
Clay began the fight against the administration's bank
policy by introducing a resolution calling on the President for a copy of his cabinet message of September 18.
This was a tactical error, for Jackson refused to grant the
request, standing on his constitutional rights. On December 26, Clay then presented his famous resolutions of
censure of the President. The first of these declared that
the President's dismissal of Duane and the appointment
of Taney for the express purpose of removing the government deposits constituted an assumption of power over
the Treasury "not granted to him by the Constitution
and the laws, and dangerous to the liberties of the people," while the second declared that the reasons given
by the new Secretary for the removal policy were "un-
satisfactory and insufficient."

Clay accused Jackson and his cohorts of changing the
pure republican character of the government into a tyr-
anny. There were echoes in his speech of Cicero's indictment of Cataline, of the philippics of Demosthenes, and
of Patrick Henry's arraignment of George III. He condemned Jackson for an abuse of the executive power both
in the exercise of the veto and in the employment of the
appointive and removal powers. He attacked him for dis-
regarding the decision of the Supreme Court in the
Cherokee Indian case, for preventing appropriations for
internal improvements by his veto, and for defeating the
will of the people by his pocket veto of the Distribution
bill. His main arguments were based on a rather strict in-

terpretation of constitutional law. From his study of the Federalist Papers and the debates in the ratifying conventions of Virginia and other states, he concluded that the President had no authority to interfere with a cabinet officer performing a duty in accordance with a specific law. In dictating the action of the Secretary of the Treasury in regard to the deposits, Jackson had united control over the purse and the sword. Thus he had violated a cardinal principle in a republic of the division of power and was thereby converting the President's office into an elective monarchy.

The debate on Clay's resolutions lasted over three months. Meanwhile the United States Bank had contracted its credits, producing much distress among debtors and in business circles. It was regarded by Jacksonians as a Biddle-inspired panic to force the return of the deposits and the recharter of the bank. Clay sought to utilize the economic distress of the country by advocating the exertion of pressure on Congress by numerous petitions from the people. When "Gallant Harry" directed an impassioned plea to the Vice President presiding over the Senate to intercede with the President to relieve the distresses of the people, Van Buren coolly stepped down from the chair and asked Clay for a pinch of snuff, inhaled it, and walked away. Jackson was not so urbane in his reaction to Clay's oratory. To his adopted son he wrote on February 16, 1834: "The storm in Congress is still raging, Clay reckless and as full of fury as a drunken man in a brothel, his abuse and his coadjutors pass harmless by me. The Deposites will not be removed [sic] nor the Bank rechartered."

On March 28, 1834, the Senate by a vote of 26 to 20 adopted Clay's resolutions of censure, Calhoun and Webster voting for them. In April, Jackson prepared a protest. He observed to his adopted son that he would show "that it is not I, but the Senate who have usurped power and violated the constitution, and I am sure that the people will recollect, that it was a corrupt and venal senate that overturned the liberty of Rome before ever Cezar reached her gates, and if ever our republic is overthrown it will be by a venal Senate usurping all power and forming an alliance with a corrupt monied aristocracy."

Jackson's henchman Senator Thomas Hart Benton introduced a resolution to expunge the censure from the Senate journal. The anti-Jackson coalition resisted the proposal to delete the censure as unconstitutional and a desecration of the journal of the Senate. Even one of Jackson's own supporters, Senator Hugh Lawson White of Tennessee, a man of great independence and of Roman virtue, refused to vote for the mutilation of the journal.

Clay retained a strong feeling of rancor against the autocratic President. In the spring of 1835 he found an opportunity to curb Jackson as well as to render a valuable service to the country. France had long refused to pay some legitimate claims of American citizens arising from the seizure of United States vessels, and the President had recommended the seizure of the property of French citizens in the United States to satisfy these claims if the French legislature failed to appropriate money for this purpose. Jackson's brusque threats greatly incensed the French people and produced a state of serious tension between the two countries. Clay feared that the President's belligerent course might lead to war and that he had unnecessarily insulted the French people. Accordingly, he reported a resolution declaring it "inexpedient at this time to pass any law vesting in the President authority for making reprisals upon French property." He admitted that the United States had a just grievance against France, but he believed that the wisest policy was one of delay. His report, slightly amended, was adopted unanimously.

This victory over the President was only a slight alleviation of the succession of defeats that the Kentucky statesman had suffered at the hands of Jackson's party. Clay was generally optimistic, but at this period of his life he was disillusioned. On June 25, 1835, he wrote that he saw a striking resemblance between the means and measures practiced by the Jacksonians and the evils of the Civil War in England as depicted by Clarendon in his *History of the Rebellion*. Only the religious fanaticism of seventeenth-century England, he observed, was lacking; but the fanatical subservience to Jackson took the place of that folly. All of Clay's major policies had been defeated, the recharter of the national bank, the preservation of a high tariff, the restoration of the deposits, federal appropriations for internal improvements, such as the Maysville Turnpike bill, and his Distribution bill.

This last bill Jackson had pocket-vetoed in 1833. Clay did not give up because of this rebuff, but continued to advocate its enactment in successive sessions of Congress. He was chagrined that the representatives of the Southern states voted against his proposal despite the fact that it provided for counting slaves as well as whites in the apportionment for the distribution of the profits derived from the sale of the public domain. In place of his land bill Congress in 1836 passed the Distribution of the Surplus Act. Clay reluctantly voted for this measure, which further stimulated speculation and extravagance in the states, partly because of his desire to remove the treasury surplus from the control of Jackson.

So dominant was Jackson over his party that he dictated the nomination of the presidential candidate in the Democratic Republican convention of 1836. Outraged by this autocratic course, Clay predicted that the election of

Van Buren as President would perpetuate the misrule of Jackson's administration and lead to a vast system of corruption. Despite his unceasing ambition to be President, Clay was convinced that it was useless to run against Van Buren and therefore he did not offer himself as a candidate nor did he take any active part in the campaign. He voted for William Henry Harrison because he regarded him the most likely of the opposing candidates to upset Van Buren. The victory of the New Yorker was discouraging to a man with Clay's views of republican virtue, who looked upon the Jacksonians as modern Goths.

The crowning act of humiliation for him was the success of the movement to expunge the censure of Jackson which followed Van Buren's election. Thomas Hart Benton at every session of Congress since the passage of Clay's resolution of censure of the President had sought to get the Senate to rescind it. Whenever the Democrats obtained control of state legislatures they adopted the practice of instructing the senators to vote for expunging the censure from the journal. Some of the senators refused either to obey the instructions or resign, but others followed the course of Senator John Tyler of resigning rather than obeying the instructions. Shortly before Jackson retired from office, in January, 1837, Benton was able to marshal enough votes to remove the record of censure from the journal, but only after a compromise had been devised by which black lines were drawn around the censure and a statement written across the record that it had been expunged by act of the Senate.

Clay made an eloquent last-ditch plea to the Senate not to desecrate its journal by adopting Benton's resolution. In this tour de force he reviewed the controversy with Jackson over the removal of the deposits that had led to the adoption of the censure. He maintained that the President possessed no authority over the Treasury, the power of supervision belonging to Congress, and that Jackson had violated the Constitution in ordering the removal of the deposits and in dismissing a Secretary for failing to obey his orders in this respect. Clay then defended the legal right of the Senate to pass a resolution of censure of the President. In a delightful bit of irony he declared that if an American monarch should arise on the ruins of the Constitution, he might reward his followers by conferring upon them a new order of knighthood, the order of the Knight of the Black Lines. Other anti-Jackson leaders, W. C. Preston, Calhoun, and Webster, spoke to hushed audiences in the Senate describing the awful crimes of expunging. But Benton had rounded up the votes, and in a dramatic session of the Senate he secured the passage of the expunging resolution by a vote of 24 to 19. Before the act of expunging was consummated, all the opponents of the measure except Senator Hugh Lawson White filed out from the Senate Chamber in order not to witness this act of desecration.

Clay now found service in Congress, which had formerly been so exhilarating, very repugnant to him. In February, 1835, he wrote, "I am truly sick of Congress." At the end of the year he was saddened by the death of his cherished daughter Anne. To his friend Brooke he lamented, "Blackguards, Bankrupts and Scoundrels, Profligacy, and Corruption are the order of the day." After the expunging resolution had passed, he declared, "The Senate is no longer a place for any decent man." Nevertheless, when the legislature of Kentucky re-elected him to the Senate, he accepted the position.

In concerting the principal measures of opposition against Jackson's administrations Henry Clay had taken the lead. Webster and Calhoun had cooperated, but Clay was the effective leader of the opposition forces in Congress. The personality of Jackson was so dictatorial and passionate, his hates and loyalties were so strong, and his reactions to political issues were so personal, that he greatly accentuated partisanship in American politics. He alienated men who were disgusted with his use of the spoils system and his free use of the veto power. His veto of the Maysville Turnpike bill incensed a strong group in the West that desired the government to adopt a policy of federal aid for internal improvements. He alienated another powerful group by his stern measures in suppressing the nullification movement. His harsh Indian removal policy turned others into opposition. Perhaps the bank policy of Jackson, particularly his removal of the deposits, was the most important catalytic agent in coalescing various incongruous elements of opposition into a new political party. At first there was no formal organization of the party, but the opponents of Jackson began to call themselves "Whigs" after the English party that sought to curb the power of the king. Cartoonists represented Jackson as King Andrew I with a crown on his head, wearing an ermine robe and holding a scepter in his hand.

Clay first used the term Whig in a speech in the Senate on March 14, 1834, describing the distressing effects on the country caused by the removal of the deposits. He spoke of the Whigs as the champions of liberty while he sought (unsuccessfully) to affix upon the supporters of Jackson the opprobrious term of Tory. The hard core of the Whig party was the business interests of the North, the protariff, probank men who had voted for Clay in 1832 when he was the National Republican candidate for President. This group, with the exception of his Kentucky supporters, remained his most devoted followers throughout his political career. After he was defeated for the Presidency in 1844 the merchants of New York held a meeting, presided over by Philip Hone, the diarist, for the purpose of raising funds to erect a statue of Clay (by Crawford) to be placed in "the rotunda of the Merchants' Exchange or some other suitable place." The "mill-boy of the Slashes" had become the leader, not of the democratic masses, but of the party whose dominant element belonged to the broadcloth class.

The Whigs were strong in the cities and towns. Clay expressed surprise in 1839 that "in our Cities, where we had most to apprehend from political corruption, we have found most public virtue; whilst in the Country, where we had a right to expect most opposition to misrule, and wild and dangerous theories, they have received an alarming degree of countenance." In the South the Whigs were frequently wealthy aristocratic planters, particularly sugar planters and businessmen. But there were also humble men in the hills and mountains of the Alleghenies who were swept into the Whig ranks during the log cabin and hard cider campaign of 1840. One of the humble people who became an ardent Whig was the free Negro John Chavis, schoolmaster of a white school in Raleigh, North Carolina, attended by children of the most eminent families of the state. In 1833 he wrote to his former pupil Senator Willie P. Mangum, "I have long believed Clay to be a tryed and faithful patriot and I think his Tariff question proves it beyond a doubt. . . ." Nonetheless, Clay's party was pre-eminently the party of wealth and conservatism in America.

V I I I

The Humanitarian

CLAY SPENT much of his life battling for property rights, yet his kindly nature responded sensitively to the humanitarian movement in America of the 1820's and 1830's. Clay was a humanitarian but not a reformer, certainly not one of the New England type. He abhorred the "isms" championed by crusaders such as Orestes Brownson, Theodore Parker, and William Lloyd Garrison. His type of humanitarian feeling, closer to paternalism than to reform, was revealed in his recommendations as to a just Indian policy and his efforts in behalf of the emancipation of the slaves. As a young man, he had held the office of prosecuting attorney briefly and had prosecuted a slave for killing a brutal overseer who had whipped him. He succeeded in having the slave convicted and hanged. In talking with George D. Prentice, his earliest biographer, Clay said that he regretted his part in the execution of the poor slave "more than any other act of his professional career," and after this episode his eloquent voice was used only in the defense of accused clients.

In John Quincy Adams's cabinet at the end of December, 1825, there was a discussion of Indian affairs arising from Georgia's demand that the Creeks cede their lands within her borders. Secretary of War James Barbour proposed a plan of incorporating the Indians within the states, ceasing to make treaties with them, and extending the jurisdiction of the states over them. Clay thought that this plan was impracticable, for, he said, it was impossible to civilize Indians. The ideas which he expressed at this time were those of an extreme racist. Adams reported him as shocking Barbour by his sentiments: "He believed they [the Indians] were destined to extinction, and, although he would never use or countenance inhumanity towards them, he did not think them, as a race, worth preserving. He considered them as essentially inferior to the Anglo-Saxon race, which were now taking their place on the continent. They were not an improvable breed, and their disappearance from the human family will be no great loss to the world."

When the governor of Georgia during the following year began to survey the Indian lands, thereby violating the Treaty of Washington, the Creeks resisted and presented a grave problem of what the federal government should do. In a cabinet meeting of January 27, 1827, Clay urged, according to Adams's diary, the necessity of the federal government's protecting the rights of the Indians by force. Finally, however, he conceded that it would be better to accomplish this purpose by civil process and proposed referring the whole subject to Congress.

Clay's advocacy of the rights of the Southern Indians, while sincere, was given animus by his opposition to Jackson. In 1819, while condemning Jackson's invasion of Florida, he severely censured the latter's execution of some Indian chiefs as an instrument of retaliation, and he strongly criticized the excessively severe Indian treaty made at Fort Jackson. In the summer of 1830 Clay proposed that meetings be held in Kentucky and other states to protest Jackson's veto of the Maysville Turnpike bill and his harsh Indian policy. He advocated that the Senate should reject Indian treaties that were unjust and disgraceful to the nation. "Of all the acts of the present administration none will give you more pain to record than that relating to the Indians," he wrote. When the United States engaged in a long and costly war in the 1830's and 1840's to expel the Seminoles from Florida, Clay spoke out in the Senate against the inhumanity of the war, the waste of money, and the mismanagement of this effort to subdue the Seminoles.

On February 4, 1835, Clay made his most important speech in the Senate on the harsh treatment of the Indians by the people of the United States. He presented a memorial from a small portion of the Cherokee nation who desired to emigrate to the West and to secure the guarantee of permanent possession of their territory and self-government. Clay reviewed various treaties with the Cherokees, beginning in 1775, in which the United States Government had guaranteed their rights to their land. He then exposed the unjust laws of Georgia taking their lands away from them and extending her laws over them. He protested against the wrongs perpetrated against a part of the human race, who, although they might be destined to extinction or absorption in the white race, should be treated with "the utmost kindness and the most perfect justice." Finally he introduced resolutions to protect the Indian tribes in the possession of their lands and their treaty rights by the federal courts and to make further provision by law for setting aside a district west of the Mississippi River for those Cherokees who wished to migrate and at the same time securing these lands in perpetuity to the emigrants and their descendants.

By far the most significant manifestation of humani-

tarian sentiment by Clay was his long-continued advocacy
of the gradual emancipation of the slaves. Shortly after
he came to Kentucky Clay agitated for the calling of a
constitutional convention in 1799 to adopt a plan of
gradual emancipation for the state. The aspiring young
lawyer contributed some effective propaganda for the
cause of emancipation by letters published in the
Kentucky Gazette under the pen name "Scaevola." He declared that the conservatives who opposed any disturbance of the institution of slavery feared that the adoption of a plan of gradual emancipation might be the
entering wedge in an attack on other forms of vested interest. Sarcastically he commented that should a plan of
emancipation be initiated, "We are not sure but we may
afterwards proceed further and emancipate all the hogs in
the state or divide them among ourselves." These letters
reflected the Virginia liberalism of his old patron George
Wythe and of Thomas Jefferson, the belief that slavery
was inconsistent with the natural rights of man. In the
contest over emancipation in Kentucky in 1798-1799, the
conservatives were overwhelmingly victorious. Raising
"the whine of interest," they attacked the reformers such
as Clay as visionaries, "beardless boys" who were seeking
to advertise themselves.

Clay's attitude toward slavery may be characterized as
a practical acceptance of the institution and a theoretical
opposition to it. In 1799, the year that he married Lucretia Hart, he owned no slaves, but in the following year
he was listed in the Fayette County Tax Lists as owning
three slaves. In the Thomas J. Clay Papers in the Library of Congress is an interesting bond signed by
Thomas Hart, Jr., his brother-in-law, dated January 7,
1802, by which Hart contracted to hire three Negro
boys owned by Clay — Sam, at the price of 20 pounds
per annum, Aaron, 15 pounds, and Simon, 7 pounds —

for a period of five years, during which time he obligated himself to teach them "the trade of nailing." After
he had acquired the nucleus of Ashland in 1805 he was
assessed for the ownership of eight slaves. Thereafter he
bought and sold Negroes as needed. Clay was not averse
to buying small Negro children, as illustrated by a note
to his friend Judge Francis Brooke of Virginia in 1832:
"Could I purchase in your neighborhood a negro boy
ten or twelve years old at a reasonable price. I want
such a one to ride out a Maltese Jack." At the very end
of his life, while he was in Washington, one of his
Negro men died from smallpox. Clay thereupon sent
instructions to hire a slave as a replacement if possible,
but if one could not be hired to buy a Negro man.

Clay's ambitions and his marriage to Lucretia Hart
allied him to the slaveowning aristocracy of the Bluegrass. He could hardly escape being involved in the ownership of slaves. The use of slaves as domestic servants
was regarded almost as a necessity in upper-class families.
To operate the hemp and stock plantation of Ashland,
slave labor also was virtually indispensable. His obligations as a lawyer brought him constantly into contact
with the property aspect of slavery. In 1811, for example,
as trustee of an estate, he advertised the sale at public
auction in front of the Kentucky Hotel, which he owned,
"upwards of twenty likely slaves, being men, women,
girls, and boys."

As the proprietor of Ashland Clay was undoubtedly
a kind master. The number of slaves on the plantation
fluctuated considerably, the largest at any time being
sixty in 1846; at Clay's death there were fifty. Clay was
thus one of the large slaveholders of Kentucky, a border
slave state in which the largest slave proprietor in 1850,
Robert Wickliffe, owned only two hundred slaves. Clay
built comfortable brick cabins for his slaves, which a

visitor to Ashland in 1845 described as follows: "The houses of his slaves are all very neat, and surrounded by better gardens, and more flowers and shrubbery than one-half of the farm houses in the country, and all the inmates are as happy as human beings can be." Clay was very considerate of the feelings of his servants: for example, in 1833 he instructed his overseer to hire Abraham to a firm of Lexington hemp manufacturers, but only if he was willing to go into their employment. He bought slaves to unite families and he allowed slaves to visit their relatives in Virginia and Maryland. In 1842 a Quaker at Richmond, Indiana, presented to him a petition to free his slaves. In reply Clay said that of his slaves some half dozen from age or infirmity would not be able to earn a living in freedom, others were young and helpless, and still others would not accept freedom if offered to them. "My slaves," he said, "are as well fed and clad, look as sleek and hearty, and are quite as civil and respectful in their demeanor, and as little disposed to wound the feelings of any one as you are."

Yet there was another side to this idyllic picture, the story of runaways and of the authority of the overseer. However well treated, many of the slaves wished to be free. Clay did not in the vigorous period of his life hesitate to try to capture runaways. On the other hand, in his old age, when his servant Levi left him at Buffalo, he was philosophical. "I will take no trouble about him, as it is probable that in a reversal of our conditions, I would have done the same thing."

The case of "Black Lotty," or Charlotte, is an intriguing story of one of Clay's slaves and his relations to her. Lotty was born on the Eastern Shore of Maryland from a slave mother who later was liberated. She was brought to Lexington by a tailor who sold her to Clay in 1806 as a result of "her own pressing solicitation," for

she was married to Aron, a slave at Ashland. Clay paid
a high price of $450 for her to unite the slave family.
Later he took her and Aron to Washington to serve his
family while they were living in the city. During her
stay at the capital Clay permitted her to visit her relatives in Maryland for several weeks. In February, 1829,
Clay was forced to defend a suit in the Circuit Court of
the District of Columbia brought by Lotty for her freedom and the freedom of her two children. In replying
to this petition Clay said that he had never had the re-
motest suspicion that Charlotte was entitled to her freedom and that he believed the suit was brought to injure
him politically just as he was about to leave Washington
for Kentucky. The case was eventually decided against
Lotty, and on September 10, 1830, Clay wrote to an
agent in Washington approving his order to imprison
Lotty until she could be sent to Kentucky. He observed
that she had been her own mistress for eighteen months
since she had brought a groundless suit against him, that
"her conduct has created insubordination among her relatives here," and that it was high time to put a stop to
such conduct by forcing her to return to her duty at
Ashland.

Clay's emancipation of Lotty in 1840 was only one of
several emancipations. Anne Irwin, Clay's favorite daughter, wrote her mother from Louisiana in 1832 that she
was grateful for the use of Lotty, "the best creature I
ever saw and appears to be quite as much attached to
the children as she ever was to yours." Lotty was the
"mammy" at Ashland and in emancipating her and her
daughter Mary Anne at the same time Clay based her
emancipation "in consideration of the long and faithful
service — and of her having nursed most of my children,
and several of my grandchildren." In the Fayette County
Deed and Order Books there are records of at least seven

emancipations of slaves made by Clay in his lifetime. Among these was that in 1844 of his bodyservant Charles, who after liberation continued to serve his master at Ashland.

Clay had another opportunity to do something practical for the antislavery cause at the time of the debates over the admission of Missouri. The Tallmadge amendment to the Missouri bill provided that no further slaves should be permitted to enter the state and that all slaves born after the admission of the state should become free at the age of twenty-five. This proposal stirred up a violent debate. Clay represented Western sentiment in opposing any restrictions on a new state that did not apply to the older states. Like the advocates of other slave states, he admitted that slavery was an evil but argued that its diffusion would ameliorate the condition of the slaves. When extremists talked of disunion Clay was alarmed for the preservation of the Union and thought of compromise, suggesting that the free state of Maine should be admitted as a balance to the slave state of Missouri. He exerted himself strenuously to secure the passage of the Thomas amendment, allowing slavery to continue in Missouri but prohibiting it in the territory north of the 36°30′ line of latitude.

Clay's attitude toward the expansion of slavery into the West was somewhat ambivalent. Fifteen years later, he recalled, he had told the Missouri delegate to "go home, enter the Convention of your state and exert yourself to establish a gradual emancipation, similar to that which Dr. Franklin prevailed upon Pennsylvania to adopt in 1779." This would imply that he favored the eradication of slavery from Missouri but only by state action, a position almost exactly the same as that of the aged Thomas Jefferson.

Clay rendered a very important service to the ultimate

compromise of the Missouri question. He was not the author of the first or major compromise drawing a line through the federal territories above which slavery was prohibited. But he devised a second compromise when the antislavery members of Congress violently protested against a provision of the Missouri constitution prohibiting the entrance of free Negroes into the state. The sectional controversy then flared up again and there was danger that Missouri would not be admitted to the Union. Clay secured the appointment of a joint committee of House and Senate to consider the Missouri problem. This committee reported a compromise previously presented by Clay, namely that the legislature of Missouri should solemnly agree that its constitution should never be interpreted to deprive any citizens from another state entering Missouri of equal rights and privileges under the Constitution of the United States. This compromise was passed by the House of Representatives by the close margin of eighty-seven to eighty-one votes, and on this condition the state of Missouri was admitted to the Union on August 10, 1821.

Clay never had any doubts as to the validity of slave property. He supported the fugitive slave laws, and he even expressed an opinion favorable to the utility of the domestic slave traders. The manuscript diary of Henry Clay, Jr., in 1831 records a conversation between his father and some Southern gentlemen who were discussing the question whether public jails in the slave states should be used, as was the custom, by slave traders to receive their human property. "The traders," Henry Clay thought, his son wrote, "act as scavengers for the public; carrying off the vicious and incorrigible to another country, where new character may be formed with better habits and propensities." In 1836, when Arkansas applied for admission into the Union as a slave state, some citizens of Philadelphia revived the old issue of the Missouri Compromise by presenting petitions against the admission of another slave state into the Union. They entrusted their petitions to Henry Clay, who presented them, but he said that he was opposed to their petition. He was in favor of faithfully observing the Missouri Compromise.

It is one of the mysteries of the antislavery movement in the United States that such slight attention was ever given to a plan of compensation to slaveholders for the emancipation of their slaves such as Great Britain worked out in 1833. The United States possessed a rich resource in the public domain which might have been used for this purpose. Clay was one, however, who considered this method of gradually getting rid of slavery. In March, 1832, shortly after the great debate in the Virginia legislature on emancipation, he suggested that since the national debt might be regarded as virtually paid, Congress should appropriate ten million dollars annually for the emancipation of the slaves in the United States. Clay was skeptical that the Southern people would approve such a radical proposition, because of the existence of a morbid feeling in regard to slavery. When he communicated to a Southern senator his desire to introduce a constitutional amendment authorizing Congress "to remove the free and purchase the bond people of color," the senator indicated that such a proposal would not be well received in his section. Since Clay usually acted on the pragmatic principle that the art of politics consisted in attempting only the possible, he made no public move to carry out his noble project.

In the 1830's Clay became progressively conservative on most political subjects. His attitude toward slavery reflected this change, just as he became less and less a representative of Western interests. In a letter of July 7,

1833, to his brother-in-law James Brown he expressed the opinion that the emancipation of the slaves in the West Indies would exert a moral influence on the institution of slavery in the United States. It would make the Southern slaveholders "more sensitive to the slightest disturbance of the question." He did not, however, apprehend any immediate effects in the United States from the abolition of slavery in the West Indies, for the North had no strong economic interest in seeking to emancipate the Southern slaves, and the leading politicians of that section were committed not to interfere with Southern slavery. He looked forward with many others "to some distant period when it would cease in the U. States but I think it will not happen in our time."

James G. Birney's diary, recording a breakfast conversation with Clay in the autumn of 1834, also illustrated the very cautious attitude Clay had developed in regard to the emancipation of the slaves. When Birney broached the subject of starting an antislavery movement, Clay maintained that slavery existed in so mitigated a form in Kentucky as not to be a great evil. He pointed out "that men's interest in property had been found an insurmountable barrier to gradual emancipation then (in 1799), that *now* they were more formidable — the case was hopeless by any direct effort and was to be left to the influence of liberal principles as they should pervade our land. He spoke of Mr. Robert Breckinridge having put himself down in popular estimation by having advocated emancipation and that he [Breckinridge] and Mr. John Green, two gentlemen of great worth, had disqualified themselves for political usefulness by the part they had taken in reference to slavery." Clay was an ambitious politician and he did not intend to disqualify himself for office.

Gradual emancipation, he thought, could be safely

adopted in states where the proportion of blacks to
whites was small — in Missouri, for instance, where the
Negroes constituted a little over one fifth of the population. Where the black population was preponderant or
nearly equal to the white, he opposed even gradual
emancipation. He had then accepted the doctrine that
the South was to be a "white man's country," although
significantly he warned his correspondent that his views
were "not for publication."

At all times Clay, in common with other Southern
liberals on the slavery question, was opposed to the immediate emancipation of the slaves. "It could not be
adopted justly without compensation, and could not
safely, considering the want of qualification in the slaves
either to enjoy freedom or provide comfortably for themselves."

The development in 1835-1836 of the abolitionist
strategy of presenting petitions to Congress to abolish
slavery in the District of Columbia and in the federal
territories led to a great controversy over the freedom of
petition. The extreme defenders of slavery, led by Calhoun in the Senate, were opposed even to receiving the
petitions. The House of Representatives passed a gag
resolution in 1836 providing for receiving abolitionist petitions but immediately tabling them. The Senate did
not resort to such an undemocratic procedure as a standing rule, but regularly voted to receive and then table
such petitions. Regarding the abolitionists as a very small
element of the Northern population, Clay wished to
avoid giving these zealots an opportunity to ally their
cause with the issue of the freedom of petition and debate. Consequently, he was in favor of not only receiving their petitions but referring them to the proper committee, the Committee on the District of Columbia, "to
act on them as they pleased." When Southern congressmen

argued that the reception of the abolitionists' petitions would lead to endless debate, Clay replied that this objection was not a valid excuse for denying the right of petition. Debate, argument, reasoning were essential to a democratic system of government and should not be repressed. This same attitude caused him to vote against Calhoun's bill of 1836 excluding from the mails any publications which states prohibited from circulating in their borders.

Calhoun and Clay engaged in an intellectual duel at the end of December, 1837, over some resolutions on slavery which the South Carolinian introduced in the Senate. Clay considered them a political maneuver to advance Calhoun's political ambitions. He retorted by introducing a counterresolution that the Senate had a duty to preserve the constitutional right of petition and was bound to receive and treat with respect petitions concerning slavery in the District of Columbia. Believing that Congress had jurisdiction over slavery in the District of Columbia and in the federal territory of Florida, he was willing to receive petitions concerning them. On the other hand, he advocated the instant rejection of petitions concerning the abolition of slavery in the states, for he believed that Congress had no jurisdiction over that subject.

In 1837 there appeared a small cloud on Clay's political horizon — the Texas question. In replying to the poet and abolitionist John Greenleaf Whittier on July 22, Clay said that the annexation of Texas should not be determined with reference to whether such an action advanced or injured the slave interest in the United States. He believed that if a large portion of the people of the United States opposed annexation this fact ought to be the great, if not conclusive, consideration for rejecting Texas. At the same time, he expressed his strong feeling that the agitation of the immediate emancipation of the slaves by the abolitionists was highly injurious to "the slave himself, to the master, and to the harmony of the Union."

At the close of the year Clay expressed a similar view of the abolitionists in a letter to James G. Birney, who tried to enlist the great statesman in a movement to abolish slavery in Kentucky. Birney had deplored the recent decision of his native state against calling a constitutional convention, which he interpreted to be a setback for the antislavery cause. Clay replied: "Will you believe me, when I assure you that it is my clear conviction that the decision against a convention was mainly produced by the agitation of the question of Abolition at the North? I will not say that, without that agitation this State was ripe for gradual emancipation, but it was rapidly advancing to that point. We are thrown back fifty years." The recent movement to call a constitutional convention in Kentucky, Clay said, he had opposed because he did not believe that there was the slightest prospect of carrying any antislavery scheme even of gradual emancipation in the state.

When the Southern leaders in the 1820's and 1830's began to justify slavery as a positive good, Clay vigorously dissented. To a correspondent in Alabama he wrote in 1838: "I am no friend to slavery. I think it an evil; but I believe it better that slaves should remain slaves than to be set loose as free men among us. That is our true ground of defense. That was the ground of our Revolutionary Ancestors. But the modern ground assumed by the new school in South Carolina that slavery is a blessing is indefensible, unintelligible, and brings reproach upon us. If slavery is a blessing, the more of it the better and it is immaterial, upon that hypothesis, whether the slaves be black or white."

Clay always maintained that his position on emancipation never changed from that taken by him in 1798-1799. He was never in his whole life, he said, in favor of immediate freeing of the slaves, but of a cautious emancipation where the proportion of the slaves to the white population was small. He would be opposed to emancipation where there might be "danger of the blacks acquiring the ascendancy."

The rise of the abolition movement in the North cast a shadow over Clay's prospects of becoming President. When Birney wrote him that the election of a slaveholder to that office would be a public calamity, Clay protested, pointing out that such a rule would have deprived the country of the services of Washington, Jefferson, Madison, and Monroe as chief executives and of John Marshall as Supreme Court Justice. To his Virginia confidant, Francis Brooke, he expressed a fear that there was danger of proscribing slaveholders from being elected to federal office. The success of the abolitionists in this respect would lead to "other encroachments," such as the enactment of a law prohibiting the interstate slave trade, then the abolition of slavery in the District of Columbia, and finally, "the end will be ——." Later, Clay commented bitterly that in his campaigns he was attacked by the abolitionists as a proslavery man and by the ultra-Southern men as an abolitionist.

In 1839 Clay looked forward to being nominated by the Whigs for President. It was important that he should reassure the South that he was not hostile to slavery. On February 7 a major speech in the Senate set forth his views on the abolitionists and on the proper relation of the national government to slavery. Moderate in tone, his speech was an appeal to the intelligence rather than to the emotions, having something of the stateliness of an oration of Demosthenes. The free states, he maintained, had no more power to intermeddle with slavery in the Southern states than to interfere with the internal institutions of a foreign country. A nationalist in his economic views, Clay was a stanch state rights man in matters relating to slavery.

The ultimate end of the abolitionists, he declared, was the overthrow of slavery in the states and if they succeeded in attaining their objective, a violent war would result between the whites and the blacks that would lead to the extermination or subjugation of one race or the other. Clay also pointed to the immense loss of property that would attend the immediate emancipation of the slaves and he maintained the rightfulness and legality of this property. If the abolitionists were seriously determined to accomplish their purpose, he said, they should raise a fund of twelve hundred million dollars assessed entirely upon the free states. The abolitionists had thrown back the cause of gradual emancipation half a century, he believed, and their agitation had increased the rigors of legislation controlling the slaves in the Southern states. Clay observed that if the abolitionists succeeded, large numbers of the blacks would migrate to the free states to compete with the white laboring population. Finally, he made a plea to Northerners to stop the reckless course of the abolitionists, which would lead inevitably to the dissolution of the Union.

Clay was very pleased with the reaction of his Northern friends to the speech. That Clay, as candidate for President, had made an important concession to proslavery interests was recognized by Calhoun, who arose in the Senate to compliment him on his speech. The great high priest of the proslavery cult in the South pointed out the change that had come over Clay since 1837, when he had opposed Calhoun's resolutions on slavery. It was humiliating for Clay to sit quietly while Calhoun associ-

ated this speech with his own resolutions in advancing
"the great moral revolution" in the South whereby Southerners no longer apologized for but recognized that this
Southern institution was a blessing. It was ironical also
that Clay's famous pronouncement "I had rather be right
than be President" was occasioned, according to his close
friend Senator William C. Preston of South Carolina, by
the delivery of this speech. When Clay consulted with
Preston and other friends, the South Carolinian told him
that his speech might be condemned by ultra men in both
parties. He replied with the famous sentiment that has
so often been quoted as evidence of Clay's lofty devotion
to principles over expediency.

Three years later, he had not changed his views. The
mass of abolitionists, he believed, were sincere but were
deluded by their leaders, who wished to rise into political
office. The ultimate fate of slavery would depend on an
all-wise Providence. Already, he noted, steps had been
taken to rid the nation of this historic evil, such as the
prohibition of the slave trade, the gradual abolition of
slavery in the Northern states, the fact that some of the
slave states had begun seriously to think of gradual emancipation at a time when the intemperate zeal of the
abolitionists checked such a movement, the amelioration
of the slave code, and finally, the progress of the American
Colonization Society. Clay's advice was that of the conservative, namely to cease agitation of a subject which threatened to destroy the Union and to leave the question of
emancipation to posterity.

Clay's ownership of slaves placed him at times in a
most embarrassing position. In passing through Richmond, Indiana, in the fall of 1842 he attended a large
Whig rally at which a Quaker named Mendenhall presented to him a petition urging him to free his slaves. A
candidate for the Presidency, Clay averted this blow in

a masterly manner. Ironically he alluded to the lack of courtesy shown to him, a stranger passing through Richmond as a result of an invitation on the way to his duties at Washington. In reply to the petition he said that although he was opposed to slavery he believed that the immediate abolition of the institution would lead to race conflict and to the extermination or expulsion of the blacks. Like virtually all Southerners, he spoke with violent aversion of the prospect of an amalgamation of the blacks and whites, which, to his mind, immediate abolition threatened. In the slave states, he declared, such strong feelings existed on this subject of intermarriage that "no human law would enforce a union between the two races." He closed by raising an embarrassing question for the abolitionists. If he freed his fifty slaves at Ashland, whom he estimated to be worth fifteen thousand dollars, he asked would Mendenhall raise an equal sum to care for the liberated slaves?

Clay was deeply disturbed by the split in the Methodist Church over slavery in 1844. He felt that this schism, by placing the free states in one camp and the slave states in another, weakened the bonds of the Union. To Dr. W. A. Boothe he wrote, "My opinion is that the existence of slavery, or the *fact* of owning slaves in States which authorize the institution of slavery, does not rightly fall within the jurisdiction of Ecclesiastical bodies."

Henry Clay's solution to the slavery and the race problem in the United States was colonization. Clay presided over the first organization meeting of the American Colonization Society in Washington on December 28, 1816, and he later served as president of the society. In a speech to the society on January 20, 1827, he proposed that both the states and the federal government should make appropriations to aid the cause of colonizing free Negroes in Africa. He argued that the vacuum of labor created by the removal of the blacks would be filled by intelligent white immigrants and that the colonization movement was a definite step toward gradual emancipation. He pointed out that colonization would remove the most vicious element of the Negro race in America, the free Negroes; and yet in strange contradiction, he said it would send the Negroes as missionaries to carry Christianity to the Dark Continent. One of the blessings of colonization, he wrote in a letter to the Reverend John White, was that it afforded the most encouraging hope in the future against the amalgamation of the black and the white races. "The God of nature," he declared, "by the differences of color and physical constitution, has decreed against it." Clay maintained in 1827 that colonization was feasible, using statistics to show that the increase of slaves had been only three per cent annually, that shipping for transportation of the slaves would employ only one ninth of the mercantile marine of the United States, and that the cost was small in comparison with the immense benefits to be derived from removing a great evil.

Henry Clay's humanitarian feelings in respect to the emancipation of the slaves had often been held in check by his political ambitions. But the rejection of him by the Whigs as a candidate for the Presidency in 1848 seems to have caused him to abandon all hope of attaining the cherished ambition of his life. He was then seventy-one years old. In the summer of 1848 the people of Kentucky had voted for the calling of a constitutional convention. The election of delegates to the convention was set by the legislature for August, 1849, and the convention was to assemble on the first Monday in October. A great agitation occurred during this period in favor of the adoption of a plan of gradual emancipation of the slaves. Only three years before, the people of Lexington, headed by Henry Clay's son James B. Clay, had suppressed the antislavery newspaper the *True American,* edited by Clay's cousin Cassius Marcellus Clay. The fiery antislavery editor felt bitter toward his distinguished cousin for his neutrality during the episode. He accused Henry of departing from Lexington on August 14, the day of the mob, for the Virginia springs, refusing to remain in the town to save his kinsman's life. But now the emancipation movement had again become respectable; many prominent Kentuckians supported it; and two newspapers, the Lexington *Examiner* (a successor of the *True American*) and the *Courier,* both published at Louisville, gave their active support.

Thus the stage was set for the appearance of Clay's famous Pindell letter of February 17, 1849. Clay at that time was in New Orleans. Purged of his ambition to become President, he still had a desire to return to the Senate and he knew that his friends were seeking to secure his election in the General Assembly. Nevertheless, he wrote the Pindell letter proposing that Kentucky should adopt a plan of gradual emancipation by which slaves born in the state after 1855 or 1860 should be free upon attaining the age of twenty-five years. An indispensable part of his program was his recommendation that the freed Negroes should be sent to Africa. The expense of the voyage and the provision of an outfit, he suggested, would be defrayed by the requirement that the slave should be hired during the last three years of his bondage and his wages set aside for this purpose.

Clay sought in this letter, which he intended for publication, to refute the proslavery philosophy. He declared that the argument advanced by the proponents of this philosophy based on "the alleged intellectual inferiority" of the African race to the white race proved too much. Such a philosophy would justify a superior white nation in subjugating and reducing to slavery backward white peoples, and, carried to its logical extreme, would entitle the wiser and more cultivated individuals of a white society to enslave the less fortunate members. In addition to his philosophical argument Clay pointed out that Kentucky was essentially a farming rather than a planting state and therefore had different economic interests from those states which were engaged in cultivating cotton and sugar. She should not be influenced too much, therefore, by the objection that his plan of emancipation would separate Kentucky from the other Southern states.

Clay anticipated that his letter on emancipation would be unpopular in Kentucky and in the Southern states generally. He wrote to his son James from New Orleans that he regretted to hear that it was not popular. "I suppose that my letter will bring on me some odium. I nevertheless wish it published. I owe that to the cause, and to myself, and to posterity."

When Clay returned to Lexington, he entered into the campaign to elect emancipation delegates to the constitutional convention. On April 25 he presided over an emancipation convention held at Frankfort of representatives from various parts of the state. But he had little hope that any plan of emancipation would be adopted at this time. "This inauspicious state of things," he believed, "is to be ascribed to the indiscreet and unwise interference on the subject of slavery by violent abolitionists in other states, to the jealousy existing between the two rival parties of Whigs and Democrats in Kentucky, and to the timidity of leading individuals among us, in suppressing their real sentiments." His pessimism was justified, for despite the great agitation not a single emancipation delegate was elected to the constitutional convention and the convention strengthened the bonds of slavery in Kentucky.

A few months before he died in 1852, the old statesman expressed his disillusionment in a letter recommending the recognition of the independence of Liberia by the United States. It was too much to hope for the possibility of establishing a system of gradual emancipation of the slaves of the United States. "After the failure of the experiment in Kentucky two years ago, I confess I despair of obtaining the object by legal enactment. I nevertheless confidently believe that slavery will ultimately be extinguished when there shall be a great increase of our population, and a great diminution in the value of labor." Thus he wrote *finis* to a chapter of cautious liberalism in his own life and in the life of a persistent minority of Kentuckians.

His will, dated July 10, 1851, did not free outright any of his slaves. He partitioned them among his family with the stipulation that if any of his servants should be sold, families should not be separated without their consent. But his will was faithful to his long-cherished devotion to colonization. It provided that all children born of his female slaves after January 1, 1850, should be liberated, the males at twenty-eight and the females at twenty-five years of age, and sent to Liberia. The expense of transportation and of an outfit should be earned by hiring the prospective freemen for three years prior to their emancipation. Furthermore, his will required that they should be taught to read, write, and cipher. This document illustrates Clay's genuine interest in humanitarianism; at the same time it reveals his sense of moderation, which made it difficult for him to take the extreme positions that politics called for in the last decade of his life.

I X

The Irony of Politics

ON MARCH 11, 1837, James Fenimore Cooper, the novelist, wrote to his wife describing a debate between Calhoun and Clay, "an intellectual duello — one of those pitiful personal wranglings, in which a day was lost humoring the vanity and self-consequence of two men." Although Cooper's criticism contained a measure of truth, he did not see that Calhoun, Clay, and Webster were spokesmen in the Senate of powerful economic and sectional groups. Calhoun sought to establish an interpretation of the Constitution which would protect the economic interest of the Southern slaveholders. The nationalism of Clay and Webster benefited the business interests of the Northeast. After the panic of 1837 the mood of the country was for a change from the Jackson-Van Buren hegemony, and the stage was set for the victory of the Whig party and the dictatorial leadership of the Kentucky Senator.

Clay had thought very well of Calhoun during the seven years that the Carolinian fought shoulder to shoulder with him to curb the power of Jackson. But in 1837 Calhoun rejoined the Jacksonians and supported Van Buren's independent treasury scheme. Then "Gallant

Harry" became suddenly aware of Calhoun's great deficiencies. Clay, Calhoun, and Webster were very ambitious to become President, and Martin Van Buren was quite anxious to be re-elected President in 1840. This rivalry strongly colored the political activities of all these men, made them suspicious of each other, and distorted their judgments. Calhoun shrewdly analyzed the compromising nature of the two most powerful of his rivals: "The two prominent candidates [for President] Mr. Van Buren and Mr. Clay naturally come together on all questions on which North and South come into conflict. One is a Southern man relying on the North for support, and the other a Northern man relying on the South. They of course dread all conflicting questions between the two Sections, and do their best to prevent them from coming up, or when up to evade them."

Calhoun deliberately threw a firebrand into the relatively peaceful situation when on December 27, 1837, he introduced into the Senate some resolutions stating the compact theory of the Constitution and an extreme position in the defense of slavery. Clay described them as "five or six as abstract resolutions, as a metaphysical mind can devise." Their real aim was to advance Calhoun's political interests. By reviving and rallying the state rights party, they set a trap for the Kentuckian to injure him with the voters of the South. Clay resolved to avoid the danger by comporting himself in such a way that he would lose favor neither in the North nor the South.

He counterattacked, first by introducing a compromise; then, about a month later, by answering Calhoun's speech in favor of the independent, or sub-treasury, scheme. Clay worked hard on this forensic effort and he was very excited over it. To his son he wrote shortly after he had delivered it, "My health is not good. I am worked almost to death.

Last Monday I spoke upwards of four hours. I never was better satisfied with any Spech [*sic*] I ever made."

This polemic, of which Clay was so proud, had two main parts. Clay reviewed the history of the destruction of the Second Bank of the United States, which he attributed to the egotism and vanity of Jackson. He maintained that Jackson and Van Buren had tried to pull down the whole banking system of the United States, including state banks, and to set up upon its ruins a government treasury bank under the exclusive control of the President. They were seeking to establish a hard-money currency of gold and silver specie. The speech, full of irony and sarcasm, was replete with references to ancient history and was marred by a bitter prejudice against Jackson.

His bold attack on Calhoun pointed out that the Senator from South Carolina and he had begun public life together and had agreed in most of their policies. But recently Calhoun had changed. "We concur in nothing now." The Carolinian had made "a summerset." Clay also spoke of Calhoun's intellectual qualities with caustic disparagement, describing his discourse as arid and metaphysical, selfishly partisan rather than patriotic. He condemned Calhoun for seeking to bring about a Union of the South rather than thinking of the national welfare.

At the end of twenty days Calhoun replied to the "Kentucky Hotspur" in an oration that was carefully elaborated and showed traces that he had freshly reread Demosthenes' "Oration on the Crown." Since the Kentucky Senator had not restricted himself to replying to his argument but had resorted to personalities, he felt justified in pointing out the defects of the honorable Senator. Clay's whole public life showed a lack of the powers of analysis and of generalization; "he prefers the specious to the solid, and the plausible to the true." Clay's weakness sprang from his lack of a sound education and his impetuous temper. "We ever find him mounted," declared the grave Carolinian, "on some popular and favorite measure which he whips along, cheered by the shouts of the multitude, and never dismounts till he has rode [*sic*] it down." Clay had thus championed first a protective tariff, then internal improvements, and finally a bank. It was a fault of his mind to seize on a few prominent and striking advantages and to pursue them eagerly without looking to consequences.

Clay continued to condemn Calhoun's agitation of Southern sectionalism. The Carolina leader, he predicted in the summer of 1838, would, despite his irreproachable private life, die a traitor or a madman. "His whole aim, at least the tendency of all his exertions of late," he wrote, "is to sow the seeds of dissention between the different parts of the Union, and thus to prepare the way for its dissolution. His little clique, distinguished more by activity and paradoxes, rather than by numbers is now busily endeavoring to propogate [*sic*] the notion that all the operations of the Federal Government, from the commencement, have been ruinous to the South, and aggrandizing to the North. This altho 40 years of the 48, during which the Government has existed, have Southern men directed the course of public affairs!" Calhoun was too rigid a personality, too much obsessed with theory and lacking common sense for Clay's taste. There was little if any fanaticism in Clay's nature; he could relax and play, but Calhoun couldn't.

Clay had clearly demonstrated his leadership of the Whigs in the Senate. The only man in the party who could be compared with him in intellectual stature and prestige was Webster. The "God-like Daniel" was a great orator but he lacked the political art and his following was largely confined to New England. After the panic of

1837 prostrated the Democratic party, Clay saw a golden opportunity to win the Whig nomination and to become President. The only danger, he felt, was a division within the party. Alarmed by an article in the Boston *Atlas* hostile to his candidacy, which he thought was inspired by Webster, he urged the Whig leaders to persuade Webster to retire from the contest.

As the campaign developed, shadows fell across Clay's prospects of securing the nomination. He became convinced that Webster was trying to turn the tide in the direction of Harrison, and he feared a boom for General Winfield Scott. There was another ominous cloud on the horizon: the entrance of the abolition movement into politics was a threat to his aspirations since he was the only slaveholder among the candidates.

Nevertheless, Clay was sanguine. He strengthened his chances of winning the Southern states, he thought, by a proslavery speech in the Senate in the fall of 1839. In the summer of that year he made a trip to Niagara Falls and then through Canada, New England, and New York. Everywhere he was received with great enthusiasm by the Whigs. Yet when he reached Saratoga, New York, among all the celebration and rejoicing there appeared the sinister figure of a powerful New York politician and wire puller, Thurlow Weed, who tried to persuade Clay to withdraw. He told the ambitious Kentuckian that three hostile forces in the North made him unavailable: abolitionism, the anti-Masonic element, and the anti-bank people. He might also have pointed out that Clay's land policy was against him in the Western states. Clay refused to listen to these warnings.

At the Whig convention which met at Harrisburg, Pennsylvania, in December, 1839, the great principle that dictated the nomination of a candidate was availability. Clay was injured by malicious rumors that he had withdrawn from the race. His enemies, politicians like Weed, succeeded in "heading him off" by getting the convention to adopt the unit rule and by working behind the scenes. Although a plurality of delegates were in Clay's favor, the seasoned politicians were able to secure the nomination of William Henry Harrison, whose availability had been indicated by the vote for President that he had received in 1836. To appease the Clay forces, the convention nominated John Tyler of Virginia, a warm friend of the "Old Prince," as the vice-presidential candidate. Because of the heterogeneous elements of the party, the Whig convention refused to frame a platform of principles.

There were two striking ironies in the political situation in 1840. The Whigs passed over their ablest man and outstanding leader for an old gentleman whose chief claim to notice was a rather dubious military record years before. The greater irony was the Whig campaign itself. A party that was essentially the party of big business in the North and of large planters in the South represented itself as the party of the humble farmer and frontiersman, using such symbols as coonskin caps, log cabins, and hard cider. Although Clay loyally supported Harrison, he thoroughly disapproved of the demagogic methods used by the Whigs to catch the popular vote. He opposed a campaign "of appealing to the feelings and passions of our countrymen rather than to their reasons and judgments." Nevertheless, he himself declared in a public speech that it was a contest between hard cider and champagne, between the log cabin and the palace.

In a notable speech in behalf of Harrison at Nashville, Clay criticized the spoils system and the appointment of corrupt men to office in Jackson's administrations. This greatly aroused Jackson, who accused Clay of demagoguery. He wrote in scorn of the Whig attempt to mislead the people "by worshiping coon and sour sider [*sic*]; the attempt by their mummeries to degrade the people to a level with the brute creation." But he erroneously thought that the people could not be hoodwinked by the Whig campaign of tomfoolery. Such appeals, he declared, were equivalent to saying to the American voters "that they are unfit for self-government and can be led by hard cider, coons, log cabins and big balls by the demagogues, as can the lowing herd be by his keeper and a baskett [sic] of salt." But the Old Hero was sadly deceived in his confidence in the sovereign people. He had not taken into account the gullibility of the voters or the effects of the financial depression. Harrison was elected by an astounding majority of 234 electoral votes to 60 for Van Buren.

Shortly after the election Harrison made a trip to Kentucky to confer with Whig leaders. The General's vanity made him morbidly sensitive lest people regard him as dominated by Clay. Yet he felt compelled to invite the Kentuckian to enter the cabinet. Clay declined, for he proposed a greater role for himself, namely, that of Whig dictator in Congress. His close friend J. J. Crittenden was appointed Attorney General, and his enemies in Kentucky, led by Charles A. Wickliffe, were kept from the rewards of the patronage. Nevertheless, Webster, who became Secretary of State, dominated the cabinet appointments. Clay's persistence in trying to secure a cabinet position for his friend John M. Clayton finally drove the exasperated Harrison to exclaim, "Mr. Clay, you forget that I am President!"

When the Kentucky Senator arrived in Washington on December 1, 1840, to take command in Congress, he was in an imperious mood, very sensitive and touchy in regard to any criticism. He strongly supported a move of the Whigs to dismiss Blair and Rives as printers for the Senate, denouncing Blair as an infamous man who for ten years had libeled him. The Democratic Senator King of Alabama replied caustically; his unfavorable comments stung Clay, who declared them false and cowardly. A duel seemed imminent, but Whig leaders brought about an adjustment. After apologizing for his violent words Clay crossed over to the seat of the Democratic leader and warmly shook hands with him. The gallery and the Senate wildly applauded this characteristic display of Clay's gift for histrionics.

Early in the session Senator Benton of Missouri introduced his famous Log Cabin bill, providing for a permanent policy of pre-emption of farms of 160 acres in the public domain at the minimum price of $1.25 an acre. Clay spoke earnestly against this measure. He maintained, with some justice, that it favored the speculators rather than the genuine log cabin people. However, by joining his own Distribution bill to the pre-emption measure, which passed on August 30, 1841, he finally secured the enactment of his cherished project. But the victory was hollow. A Democratic amendment had provided for an end to distribution when the tariff rose above twenty per cent ad valorem; and that occurred the very next year.

Unfortunately for Clay's impatient ambition to rule, the Congress elected in the fall with a working majority of Whigs in both houses would not meet until the autumn of 1841. Meanwhile Webster, in control of the cabinet, strengthened his position. The way out was to induce the President to call an extra session of Congress in the summer. Clay exerted all his power to bring this about, while Webster sought delay. The problem was complicated by the fact that the political situation in Tennessee was such that the summoning of an extra session endangered the chances of electing a Whig senator to Congress from that state. Clay, nevertheless, on March 13, 1841, demanded that Harrison call an extra session. Harrison, his

vanity touched, immediately rebuked Clay as too impetuous, pointed out that the Tennessee situation required
caution, and announced that the President must decide
the question in consultation with his cabinet.

Harrison also refused Clay's request for an immediate
personal interview. "And it has come to this!" the Kentuckian exclaimed. "I am civilly but virtually requested
not to visit the White House — not to see the President
personally, but hereafter only communicate with him in
writing. The prediction I made to him at Ashland last fall
has been verified. Here is my table loaded with letters
from my friends in every part of the Union, applying to
me to obtain offices for them when I have not one to
give, nor influence enough to procure the appointment of
a friend to the most humble position."

The unhappy Kentuckian wrote a note to the President, declaring that his enemies had prejudiced Harrison's mind against him and that the charges of dictation
were utterly unfounded. The cabinet did decide in favor
of an extra session of Congress and Harrison issued the
call for Congress to assemble on May 31. But the imperious leader of the Whigs left Washington the day after
penning his note of protest and never thereafter had a
personal conference with the President.

The breach between the President and the real leader
of the party seemed a major disaster. Then, on April 4,
the President died. Since the succeeding President, John
Tyler, was his friend, Clay believed that he could dominate the administration. But Tyler had a remarkable
sense of independence. Although he kept Harrison's cabinet, he determined to be a President in fact as well as
in name. He claimed and succeeded in establishing the
principle that the succeeding Vice President become Pres
ident and not merely the Vice President exercising the
functions of the Presidency. Tyler, like Harrison, re

sented the attempt of Clay to become the dictator of the Whig administration.

Despite the friendly relations existing between the two men at the start, a clash between Clay and the President seemed inevitable. Tyler had been nominated vice-presidential candidate of the Whig party for political expediency. He did not really belong in the party, for he was a fanatical state rights man. The Whigs should have been forewarned by his previous career of his stern devotion to his principles and of the rigidity of his mind, which was disguised by his pleasant and accommodating manner. Tyler had displayed his independence by resigning from his seat in the Senate in 1836 rather than obeying instructions of the Virginia legislature to vote for expunging the resolution of censure of Jackson. He also alone among the senators had voted against the Force bill of 1833 giving the President extraordinary powers to suppress nullification in South Carolina.

Clay, nonetheless, conceived that his position as party leader was equivalent to the position of the British Prime Minister. Accordingly, when the extra session of Congress met, he introduced a set of resolutions outlining the main measures which the Whig majority should enact into laws. They included the repeal of the independent treasury bill, the charter of a national bank, and the Distribution bill.

Most vital in Clay's mind was the bank bill. In response to a request from the Senate, Secretary of the Treasury Thomas Ewing presented a bill for the incorporation of a "Bank and Fiscal Agent" to be chartered by Congress, not in its capability as national legislature but as the local government or legislature for the District of Columbia. The bank was technically to serve the District, but it would have power to establish branches elsewhere with the consent of the states concerned. This bill was framed to meet Tyler's rigid state rights view and his denial that Congress could constitutionally charter an old-fashioned national bank. It had the support of Tyler's cabinet, of the *National Intelligencer,* the great Whig newspaper of Washington, of the moderate element of the Whig party, and of the businessmen of the Northeast. What was more important, it avoided Tyler's constitutional scruples and had therefore his acquiescence.

But Clay had different ideas as to the nature of the national bank. There was no point to an institution "having no power to branch without consent of the state where the branch is located. What a Bank *would* that be!" In an interview with the President at the opening of the extra session, he insisted upon the enactment of a bill incorporating an old-fashioned national bank. He stubbornly rejected Tyler's appeal for a bill that the latter could sign without violating his long record of consistency in opposing a national bank. Clay as chairman of the select committee to consider the charter reported a bill that carried out his ideas rather than those of Tyler. The bill provided for the incorporation of a national bank by Congress acting as a national legislature and there was no provision for obtaining the consent of the states to establish branches.

It was in this extra session of 1841 that Clay was given the title of "dictator" by his opponents and even by some of his friends. Indeed, his imperious and arrogant actions in 1841-1842 are perhaps the least defensible part of his career. He himself must have recognized this fact, for in his valedictory address to the Senate he confessed that his temper was ardent and his disposition in public service was enthusiastic; but he said those who thought he had played the role of a dictator were mistaken, they had wrongly interpreted his ardor to get legislation passed for the good of the country as evidence of dictation. His impulsiveness and his haste to enact his legislative program defeated his own ends. In order to speed the adoption of the legislative program and to avoid what he regarded as "obstruction" by the Democratic minority, he tried to get the Senate to follow the recent example of the House of Representatives in adopting, for the first time, the limitation of debate for each congressman to one hour. But this effort to restrict freedom of debate in the Senate aroused the vigorous opposition of Calhoun and Benton. Some of Clay's Whig colleagues also refused to follow him, so he abandoned the attempt.

Debate on the bank bill revealed that some of the Whigs would not vote for it as it stood; a compromise must be made. Senator William C. Rives of Virginia offered an amendment requiring the assent of the states before branch banks could be established in their limits. Although this amendment was defeated, Clay realized that some concession was inevitable. Accordingly, he accepted a modification whereby state assent was necessary, but such assent was to be assumed unless the state legislature in its first session after the adoption of the bill explicitly refused permission for a branch bank to be established. The amended bill then passed the Senate by a very slight majority. Clay even consented, in order to placate Tyler, to entitle the measure the Fiscal Bank bill. He later declared that "there was something exceedingly *outré* and revolting to my ears in the term 'Fiscal Bank' but I thought 'What is in a name?' A rose by any other name would smell as sweet." The House of Representatives also passed the bill on August 5 and it was presented to the President for his signature.

Tyler was advised by his cabinet to sign the bill, but he kept silent in regard to it until the ten-day limit had nearly expired. Then he sent a veto message to Congress, asserting that the bill violated the Constitution by en-

croaching upon state rights and by creating a national
bank authorized to loan money, a power not sanc-
tioned by the Constitution. On the evening after the veto
the jubilant Democrats paid a visit to Tyler at the White
House to congratulate him on upholding the Constitution. Clay, subsequently describing this occasion to the
Senate, composed speeches that he imagined were made
to the President by leading Democrats, particularly by
Buchanan, that were extremely ironical and amusing, revealing his gift for mimicry.

Clay's attack on the veto message emphasized a salient
point of Whig doctrine, namely, that the President should
be guided to a great degree by the advice of his cabinet
and the will of the people as expressed by the majority
of Congress. He pointed out that the Supreme Court had
in several decisions affirmed 'the power of Congress to establish a national bank. If Tyler had scruples about the
charter of a bank, he could permit the bill to become a
law without his signature or he could resign. Clay said
that if nothing could be done at the extra session to establish a bank, a way out might be found by a constitutional amendment limiting the executive veto. The old
doctrine of resistance to "executive usurpation" which
had united the Whigs in Jackson's administration might
again become a live issue before the country.

The Whigs now hastened to try to heal the breach between the President and his party by devising a new bill
that would meet his approval. The bill to establish a
"Fiscal Corporation" provided that although the new
institution could deal in bills of exchange it should not
issue discounts, to which Tyler was opposed. Clay had
nothing to do with the new measure, which represented
a genuine effort of the Whigs to conciliate the President.
Tyler pursued an ambiguous course in regard to revealing his views to the leaders of his party, possibly because

he did not wish to appear to dictate to Congress. The new bill passed Congress, but Tyler, without consulting his cabinet, vetoed it. In killing a national bank recharter Tyler probably rendered a service to his country, but at the same time he split his party. He seems to have entertained some thought that he could form a new party based on state rights that would in 1844 nominate him as its presidential candidate.

The second veto enraged the majority of the Whigs. All of the cabinet except Secretary of State Webster resigned. The latter remained loyal to Tyler, possibly because of his jealousy of Clay, but giving as his excuse that he wished to conclude negotiations then under way with the British minister, Lord Ashburton, for a treaty concerning the boundary between the United States and Canada. When Webster announced his decision to stay in the cabinet Tyler shook his hand warmly and declared, "Now I will say to you that Henry Clay is a doomed man from this hour." On the day that Congress adjourned, a large body of Whig congressmen issued an address reading the President out of the Whig party.

The crisis of the controversy had been Clay's refusal to accept the Ewing plan of a bank, which seems to have been acceptable to Tyler. The Kentucky Senator was by nature a compromiser, but on this occasion he was resolute in his drive to secure a strong national bank. He misjudged Tyler's character and persevered in his plans because he thought that Tyler would yield to the wishes of the dominant element of his party. Although Tyler had tried to dissuade Clay from pushing a bill contrary to his long-established conviction of the unconstitutionality of a national bank, the great Whig leader was uncertain what the President would do if actually presented with a strong bank bill as a *fait accompli.* Clay believed that Congress should frame a bank bill in accordance with

Whig principles to meet the needs of the country. He undoubtedly felt that he represented the Whig party in asserting the doctrine that Congress possessed broad national power, and he was willing to engage in a struggle for the supremacy of the national idea with Tyler, who represented the opposite principle of state rights. There is no evidence in the extant Clay letters that the Kentuckian desired to force Tyler to veto the bank bill in order to eliminate a rival for the Whig nomination for President in 1844. Tyler's opposition to one of the main Whig objectives seemed to Clay party perfidy.

Clay returned to Congress in the fall of 1841, but announced his intention of resigning. Of his ambitious program of legislation, only the repeal of the Independent Treasury Act and the enactment of the Distribution bill had been accomplished. To accomplish the latter, he had to support the Bankruptcy Act as a logrolling deal in order to remove the obstruction of some of the senators.

On March 31, 1842, he resigned and delivered a valedictory address that was one of the most dramatic moments in the history of the Senate. Returning to Ashland, he prepared to campaign for the Presidency in 1844. Tyler alienated the Whigs further by his vetoes, and Clay continued to accuse "His Accidency" of treason. The more vetoes Tyler now made the better; if they continued, the House of Representatives should consider the impeachment of the President.

Clay had maintained his mastery of the Whig party ever since its founding despite the fact that he had no control over the patronage. This dominance over his party, even over men like Webster, rested on a strong will, a fervid temperament, and a daring courage. Clay's appearance also aided him in impressing men. Although he did not have the Olympian gravity of the dark-visaged Daniel Webster, he had a bold, confident face, mercuri ally expressing his emotions. His greatest asset, however, was his marvelous oratorical power. His delivery and personality gave life to his speeches. Printed, they were but pale reflections of his eloquence. His voice was a magnificent instrument to express his emotions and ideas, remarkably clear, at times "soft as a lute" and other times "full as a trumpet," beautifully modulated.

The English bluestocking Harriet Martineau, a woman of fine mind but so hard of hearing that she used a huge ear trumpet, was present in the Senate in 1835 when Clay made a moving speech in behalf of the Cherokee Indians. The news that he was to speak on this subject caused foreign ambassadors to come to the Senate Chamber to hear the great orator. The galleries were crowded with gentlemen and ladies, and in the center of the lower circle stood "a group of Cherokee chiefs listening immovably." At the beginning of his speech he hesitated and appeared agitated, "shown by a frequent putting on and taking off of his spectacles and the trembling of his hands among the documents on his desk." He spoke with deliberation — he was the master of the pause — and to the English spinster his voice became "deliciously winning." His emotion mounted until Miss Martineau "saw tears, of which I am sure he was wholly unconscious, falling on his papers as he vividly described the woes and injuries of the aborigines." He made a profound moral impression upon his audience. "The chief characteristic of his eloquence," Miss Martineau judged, was "its earnestness." In speaking he gesticulated all over, using his hands, his feet, his body, even his glasses and his snuffbox to express his emotions and thoughts. An excellent mimic, he could make his audiences laugh by his caricatures of his opponents.

In contrast to Calhoun and Webster, Clay was essentially a popular orator. He appealed to the galleries by

introducing personalities in his speeches and he delighted
the common man by giving his opponents a tongue lash-
ing. Clay also indulged at times in rodomontade, Victorian sentimentalism, and grandiloquent speech. Calhoun,
on the other hand, spoke without ornament or gestures,
at a fast rate of speed, depending on an appeal to the
reason. His orations "smelt of the lamp," while the unlearned speeches of Clay had the human appeal of spon-
taneity. Yet Clay prepared some of his speeches with great
care and he buttressed his arguments frequently with
facts.

The Kentucky orator was fond of the rhetorical question,
of balanced and stately sentences, and of references to
classical history. He rarely quoted, however. When he did
attempt to repeat lines of poetry in his speeches, even familiar quotations from Shakespeare, he usually floun-
dered. His power of moving men with his oratory must
have been great. When John Randolph of Roanoke, who
had often clashed with Clay in the hall of the House of
Representatives and in the Senate, was passing through
the capital in his last days en route to Philadelphia for
medical treatment, he asked that he be taken to the Senate,
where lying on a sofa he might hear once more the marvelous voice of the great orator.

Clay's oratory must be judged in the light of the tastes
and standards of his day. Political speeches constituted
one of the favorite amusements of the rural, isolated audiences of the South and West. They liked grand effects.
They enjoyed sonorous verbiage. In the horse and coach
lays, the longer the speech the better. The manner of
presentation was often more important than the matter.
Clay responded to this taste of his age, but in his speeches
in Congress he frequently dispensed with rococo ornament and spoke in plain and simple terms, presenting
facts and solid arguments. His speeches, in fact, were less

decorated with purple patches than those of most of the admired authors of the period, such as Sergeant S. Prentiss of Mississippi. The accomplished orator was expected to transport his audience into the realm of the sublime, for this was the time of the Romantic movement. It proved also to be the golden age of American oratory.

X

An Early Victorian Gentleman

CLAY EARNED his reputation as a worldly man of pleasure, a *bon vivant,* in his early years. After he returned from Ghent in 1815 he lived in general a very decorous and dignified life. His private papers reveal not a gambler, rake, or toper, but an early Victorian gentleman. No amorous intrigues enliven the pages of his biography. Nevertheless, his political career suffered from the reputation acquired in his youth. Serious and self-righteous opponents in politics condemned him as a godless man, a drinker, a duelist, and a gambler.

In 1845 Clay replied to a peculiarly vicious and bigoted accusation made against his private life. A minister accused him of having played cards on the steamboat *Philadelphia* one Saturday night in 1830 beyond the midnight deadline, "trenching upon the Sabbath." To climax his iniquity, the Kentucky Senator had refused to attend religious services on the boat the following morning. Clay defended himself by declaring that he had made five trips on the Mississippi to New Orleans, but he had never trespassed on the Sabbath by playing cards on steamboats in his whole life. He may have refused, he admitted, to attend the sermon of a ranting, canting parson. Whist was the only game of cards, he wrote, that he had played for many years, but he had entertained himself on steamboats by the harmless pleasures of books, music, cards, and the company of ladies.

The stories about Clay's use of profanity confirmed the picture of a libertine which his enemies tried to create. His correspondence, however, contained scarcely a hint that he was addicted to this common vice of his time. No doubt he could be provoked. Clay once invited his intimate friends Robert Letcher, John M. Clayton, and Benjamin Watkins Leigh to his house to listen to a report on his Distribution bill which he proposed to present to the Senate. His guests arrived in a genial state after having dined and drunk liberally. Before he adjusted his spectacles and started to read this document, of which he was very proud, he put more wood on the fire so that the room became overheated. As he read the report in a sonorous tone for two hours, his friends, one by one, went to sleep. The loud snoring of Letcher stirred Clay to a passion and he stood in the center of the room swearing incontinently at the unlucky sleeper.

On other occasions too the emotional Kentuckian let himself go in a tirade of profanity. In the fall of 1839 Clay heard the news that intriguers in the Whig convention at Harrisburg had defeated his nomination. He was then in the parlor of his boardinghouse in Washington. "He rose from his chair, and, walking backwards and forwards rapidly, lifting his feet like a horse stringhalted in both legs, stamped his steps upon the floor, exclaiming, 'My friends are not worth the powder and shot it would take to kill them!' " His companions heard him utter "the most horrid imprecations, and then, turning to us, approached rapidly, and stopping before us, with violent gesture and loud voice, said, 'If there were two Henry Clays, one of

,hem would make the other President of the United States.' "

Clay, like the fashionable plantation gentry and politicians, was a devotee of the numerous watering resorts in the upper South. The Olympian Springs, once called Mud Lick, forty-seven miles east of Lexington, was owned at one time by his father-in-law, Colonel Thomas Hart. Henry and his family spent many pleasant months at this resort drinking the health-giving waters and inhaling the salubrious air. But most of the patrons came thither not for health but for entertainment. "There was much flirting, 'sometimes by married charmers thirsting for universal dominion.' " Clay also patronized Graham's Springs at Harrodsburg, called by enthusiasts the "Saratoga of the West," and Blue Lick Springs, both of which were easily accessible from Lexington. His favorite resort, however, was White Sulphur Springs, where he met the Whig politicians and the aristocrats from the lower South. The proprietor was an ardent Whig to whom Clay wrote not only as a tavern proprietor but as an honored friend. In his old age Clay escaped from the summer heat of Washington to Newport, Rhode Island, and Saratoga. In 1847 the old statesman went to Cape May to engage in sea bathing for the first time in his life.

Clay's health was bad through most of his political life. His letters frequently refer to severe colds and to "great debility." In 1832, when he was a candidate for President, his friend Francis Brooke became concerned over the state of his health and advised him to practice tranquillity of mind and to avoid excessive use of tobacco. Clay replied that he had quit the use of tobacco in one of the two forms to which he was addicted. But it was much harder for him to calm his fiery spirit in an election year. "Naturally ardent, perhaps too ardent," he wrote, "I can not avoid being too much excited and provoked by the scenes of tergiversation, hypocrisy, degeneracy, and corruption which are daily exhibited. I would fly from them, and renounce forever political life, if I were not restrained by a sentiment of duty, and of attachment to my friends." It is remarkable that he did not have a nervous breakdown from the strain of constant public speaking. He would make speeches of great intensity for three or four hours at a time.

Clay's personality and manners always fascinated women, even when he was an old man. In 1844 Ellen Mc-Collam, the young wife of a sugar planter, met the old statesman at a party in Louisiana, and had the honor of eating gumbo with him. Charmed, she wrote in her diary: "What a pity such a man should ever die!" The wife of Senator Josiah S. Johnston of Louisiana, Clay's campaign manager in 1832, displayed a warm affection for the Whig leader, who paid frequent compliments to her in letters to her husband. Although Clay was not an intellectual, intellectual women such as Harriet Martineau and Octavia LeVert of Mobile were strongly attracted to him. They liked his gallantry, his wit, and his agreeable manners, but perhaps most of all his highly emotional nature and his impulsiveness. Margaret Bayard Smith, whose letters were a mirror of Washington society, told how easily tears flowed from his eyes, and yet how on public occasions he could conceal his sorrows and defeats with a "mask of smiles."

While Clay was Speaker and Secretary of State in the 1820's he and Mrs. Clay entertained frequently. There was much formal visiting among official society, many stately balls and frequent dinners, fashionable levees, and drawing-room receptions. So elaborate were the costumes of women that ladies helped each other dress; Mrs. Clay and Mrs. Smith, for example, were on such intimate terms that they assisted each other. Mrs. Smith described

the Kentuckian in February, 1823, at one of these parties shortly after he had given his vote to John Quincy
Adams, "walking about with exultation and a smiling
face, with a fashionable *belle* hanging on each arm."

Some of the representatives of the plain people, such as
the Western congressman Duncan McArthur, did not
approve of these levees, so crowded that he appropri-
ately called them "squeases." All that was necessary for a
lady, he wrote, "was to have hold of some gentleman's
arm and she was perfectly secure, no matter how much
she might be pressed and squeezed on all sides by the
crowd. The fashionable manner of dressing, is to go half
necked — the neck brests and shoulder blaids bare, and
the dresses so constructed as to enable a person who
is near and above [sic] to see more than half way down
the back or front of the lady, from the upper part
of her dress. . . . This city would be the last place
that I could wish to see a wife, a daughter or female
relation. . . ."

The romantic conception of women encouraged men to
engage in the most elaborate flattery of the "fairer part
of Creation." Clay was a master of the art of courtly gallantry. There is an amusing description of his flirtation in
his old age by an obviously hostile observer. He pursued
Grace Greenwood, a vivacious and attractive young abolitionist who was visiting Washington in June, 1850. Clay
tried assiduously to convert the New England miss from
the error of her ways. But Grace Greenwood was defiant
and elusive. "Above all," her hostess wrote, "she will not
permit any of the familiarities which so many ladies seem
proud to have him take. I do not believe he will succeed
in kissing her even once. You would be amused to see how
this man's love of subduing extends even to such small
matters. He plies all the arts of flatery [sic] upon members
of Congress and very seldom fails of success." Nonethe-

less, she cherished a great admiration for "the wonderful old man!"

Grace Greenwood describes meeting him on a steamboat in New York dressed in an eccentric fashion. Her admiration for him did not prevent her from being amused at "the immensity of his long-pointed shirt collar, the shocking badness of his hat, and the utterly indescribable character of his coat," which had been made by a tailor with little attention to his shape or size. This criticism of his dress applies only to his old age. He was attentive to dress. A Whig congressman from Alabama who saw him for the first time in 1840 noted that he "wore a dress-coat of brown broadcloth, a heavy black cravat, and the collar of his shirt was of the largest size, touching his ears." Indeed, Clay was always formal in dress when away from his plantation. He refused to follow a custom that arose in the Jacksonian period of electioneering in old and ragged clothes in order to appeal to the common man.

Formality of manners and speech was a part of the romantic sentimentalism of the upper class of the South in Clay's age. This spirit also permeated his correspondence. His letters were formal and showed little evidence of the wit and humor that he displayed in the courtroom and in Congress. His correspondence gives one the impression that he consciously wrote as he conceived a dignified public man and candidate for high office should write. Consequently they make dry reading. In 1844 when Clay was a candidate for the Presidency there was a demand from his opponents that he publish certain letters which he had written to Francis P. Blair in 1825 concerning his choice for President. Clay debated with himself whether he should comply with this request but finally decided against it because they were "private and playful and written in terms of familiarity that render them unfit for the public eye."

Despite his gallantry, Clay was a faithful husband and affectionate father. His letters to Lucretia had a decidedly practical tone, but they revealed affection for her and consideration for her wishes. He sent her seed for her garden, broccoli, eggplant, and early York cabbage. He often expressed longing for her and for his Kentucky plantation. "I am sincerely and unaffectedly tired of remaining here, and wish to God that I was [sic] with you at home," he wrote from Washington. Clay sometimes wrote letters for his wife, who was "so out of the habit of writing that she even hardly ever writes to me when I am from home, leaving other members of the family to perform that office."

The domestic life of Henry and Lucretia Clay was filled with sadness as a consequence of frequent deaths among their children and of the misfortunes of those that survived. His greatest blow was the death of his daughter Anne, who had the sunny disposition of her father and was his favorite daughter. Anne died in December, 1835, while he was attending Congress. She was the last of six daughters, the others having died. To Lucretia he wrote: "If the Thunderbolt of Haven [sic] had fallen on me — unprepared as I fear I am — I would have submitted cheerfully to a thousand deaths to have saved this dear child." After this great personal tragedy, he confessed, "I feel, my dear friend, as if nothing remained for me in this world but the performance of duties."

His sons also caused Clay much sorrow. Theodore, the oldest, became insane and spent many years in the lunatic asylum at Lexington. Thomas Hart, his second son, after a period of dissipation, finally married and settled in Lexington as a hemp manufacturer, but he failed in business in 1843, owing his father $20,000 which had been advanced to him. The finest of his sons was Henry, who was graduated from West Point second in standing in his class.

He was an able young man, so devoted to his father that he tried to pattern his life after him. Yet the father's eminence overshadowed the son and he wrote in his diary in 1840, "How difficult it is for a young tree to grow in the shade of an aged oak!" The young man volunteered for service in the Mexican War, during which as a lieutenant colonel leading his troops he was killed in the battle of Buena Vista. Clay was so grateful to the officer who brought his body home that he had a gold ring made containing a lock of his dead son's hair which he presented to the officer.

Clay's tribulations did not end with the death of his promising son. There are a group of manuscript letters, recently found at Ashland, to his grandson, Henry Clay, who was a cadet at West Point. At the time of the correspondence (1850) the young Kentuckian had incurred so many demerits that he was in danger of expulsion from the academy. His grandfather begged him to redouble his efforts and to act a part "worthy of your poor father's name and mine. Imagine him to be looking down on you! How would his spirit be mortified if you dishonored him or me." Young Henry was a negligent correspondent. Clay in sending him ten dollars wrote, "Can't you get up a little earlier in the morning and write us oftener?" The last of the letters of the old statesman to his grandson, dated a few months before his death, showed his pathetic desire for letters from Henry and his concern lest he be expelled.

Clay's advice to his sons was that of a good Victorian father. He urged them to work hard, rise early, get a good education, not to gamble, and not to drink heavily. Clay seems to have been a wine drinker rather than an imbiber of Kentucky bourbon. His concept of personal liberty led him to oppose legislation prohibiting the sale of intoxicating liquors. To Harrison Gray Otis of Boston he wrote in 1839: "The Temperance cause has done great good and will continue to do so, as long as moral means are employed. But if it resorts to legislation — to coercion — it will be resisted and ought to be resisted. No man likes to have, or ought to have, cold water or brandy, separately or in combination, put in or kept out of his throat upon any other will than his own."

There was often a religious tone to Clay's letters and speeches although he did not belong to a church until the end of his life. When Anne died, he wrote to his wife that he did not have the religious resource to sustain him as she had, but that he recognized it was his duty to submit to the will of God. Clay was not skeptical of revealed religion at any period of his life. But his Baptist background led him to feel the necessity of a deep emotional experience before joining a church; and he never felt prepared for baptism until the end of his life. Nevertheless, while the cholera epidemic was raging in the country, on June 27, 1832, he offered a resolution in the Senate that the President should proclaim a fast day to invoke God's interposition. Jackson was opposed to such a proclamation as violating the principle in the Constitution of the separation between church and state, and it failed in the House of Representatives.

Clay himself blamed his failure to join a church on his absorption in worldly affairs. "Like the crowd in the active bustle of life and its varied occupations I have perhaps too much neglected so weighty a matter," he wrote in 1842. His concept of religion, like that of most of his contemporaries, revolved largely around the "preparation for a future state." The death of Henry on the battlefield of Buena Vista turned his mind to the consolations of the church, and on June 22, 1847, when he was seventy years old, he was baptized in the parlor at Ashland and became a member of the Episcopal Church.

Clay's era was sentimental and he exhibited some of

the romantic spirit of his contemporaries. His papers give no indication that he wrote poetry or indulged in composing acrostics. He shared, however, in the wave of sentimental sympathy for the Greeks when in 1821 they rebelled against the Turks. The leader of the Philhellenic movement in the United States was Edward Everett, professor at Harvard College and editor of the *North American Review*. President Monroe in two messages to Congress expressed friendship for the Greeks. On January 20, 1824, Daniel Webster introduced a resolution in the House of Representatives for the appointment of an agent or commissioner to Greece whenever the President should deem it expedient. Clay had derived a reverence for the literature of Hellas from his mentor, George Wythe. He arose in Congress and made an eloquent speech in favor of the proposal to aid the Greeks fighting for liberty.

In his public life Clay exhibited an old-fashioned type of patriotism and a scrupulous regard for the interest of the nation. A comment by Elisha Whittlesey, First Controller of the Treasury in Clay's day, illustrated this quality. Whittlesey said: "Even Mr. Calhoun has increased his charge for mileage since the old horseback and stagecoach days; and there is just one man in Congress who charges mileage as all did then. That man is Henry Clay." J. O. Harrison, Clay's executor, observed that the master of Ashland was very honorable in money matters and in keeping promises to private individuals.

Clay's personality produced widely different reactions on different observers. Hostile critics, particularly his political enemies, saw him as did Senator Armistead Mason of Virginia, who in 1816 wrote that Clay's "disgusting vanity and inordinate ambition" were fast destroying his usefulness in Washington. Andrew Jackson, who was highly suspicious of his rival for the Presidency, thought that Gallant Harry" had started and promoted the quarrel

over Peggy O'Neale Eaton in order to wreck his administration. Clay felt called upon at various times to defend
himself from the charge of vaulting ambition, but
he defied his critics to show that he had attempted to
secure the election to the Presidency "by any low or
grovelling arts — by the violation of any of the obligations
of honor."

To many observers, on the other hand, particularly
those who visited him at Ashland, Clay had a warm, frank,
and engaging personality. His son Henry, who studied his
father as a model, recorded in his diary one attribute which
made the eminent statesman so pleasing to many people.
"It is this very faculty of seeking information in conversation," he observed, "that ensures to my father his personal popularity in society. Everyone is pleased to be asked
his opinion by a distinguished individual and by thus interesting his vanity you connect yourself in a degree with his
self-love. . . ." Clay liked people and was a great admirer
of crowds. While Webster and Calhoun would cross a street
to avoid a crowd Clay would cross the street to meet one.
He was so human and affable that as he walked from his
hotel to the Capitol he greeted the slaves and common
laborers whom he met by name and chatted pleasantly with
them.

In the summer of 1837 Francis Lieber, an eminent professor of political science at South Carolina College, went
to Boston to visit his literary friends and incidentally to
buy a slave boy cheaply along the way. On his return he
stopped in Washington and talked with the venerable
Kentucky Senator, "bland noble Clay — kind as ever." As
they were conversing in the Senate Chamber, Clay turned
to Lieber and said, "I wish, my dear sir, from all my heart
that you did fill one of these chairs." Naturally the
learned professor was captivated by this great statesman.
"He took leave of me last night," Lieber wrote, "in a way

that made me feel well the whole evening. It was not that I felt flattered; it was quite different. I felt happy by his genuine and generous kindness."

Martin Van Buren, an astute observer of human nature, admired in many respects his political opponent. He liked the genial and winning personality of the Kentuckian, whom he regarded as a man of "generous impulses which were deeply implanted in his nature." Clay, he wrote, was free from the meanness of petty revenge and could on occasions rise above partisan politics to put the welfare of his country above the interest of party. Yet Van Buren thought that the Kentucky politician, in order to win partisan advantage, also resorted at times to insincere agitation, innuendo, and unfair statement. Contrasting the personalities of the two great Whig leaders, Webster and Clay, the sagacious New York politician observed that Webster was superior to the Kentuckian in intellect although Clay possessed ample powers of "close and strong reasoning," even if "he was not often inclined to exert them." Webster however was extremely selfish, underhanded, and cowardly, displaying a "habitual dread" of offending the Kentucky statesman, his rival for election to the Presidency. Clay was much above the New England orator in character and force of personality. His "physical and moral courage and . . . readiness to assume responsibility" approached "that universally conceded to his great rival Gen. Jackson."

Undoubtedly part of Clay's charm was owing to his ready wit. He did not seem to store up anecdotes as did Lincoln. But his quick mind often saw incongruous situations and made the most of them. When he first entered upon his duties as a senator in December, 1831, he was placed at "the fag end" of the Committee on Military Affairs. His friends protested at this indignity, but he replied that he was very well pleased with the position since he was a candidate for President and a military record had become the only road to political preferment. Often his wit had a sharp sting in it as when he is reputed to have said in reference to Peggy O'Neale Eaton, whose virtue had become a matter of cabinet discussion in 1830: "Age cannot wither nor time stale her infinite virginity."

Clay inspired great affection among his friends and followers. They were saddened to the point of tears when he was defeated in his candidacy for the Presidency in 1844 and they demonstrated their affection by giving him numerous gifts. Some of these were prompted by the fact that Clay was the outstanding advocate of the American System. Other gifts were the tributes of personal admiration, casks of sherry, blooded horses, socks knitted by female admirers, a silk quilt presented to him by "The Ladies of Philadelphia," buffalo tongues, a gold medal, and a gold pen. The citizens of Newark, New Jersey, gave him a high coach trimmed in red of which he seems to have been immensely proud, a symbol that a poor boy had arrived to prosperity.

The people of Kentucky and the citizens of Lexington were intensely proud of "Prince Hal," as some of them called him. They saw him acting in various situations, attending the commencement of the Lexington female academy, serving as a judge at the agricultural fair, speaking before the jury and at barbecues, acting the host at Ashland, taking his place in the line at a fire to relay the leather water buckets, talking with farmers about crops and horses and cattle, and everywhere sincerely practicing the democratic manners of a Southern gentleman. Jefferson's grandnephew Dabney Carr Terrell, who was practicing law at Louisville in 1825, expressed the admiration for Clay felt by many Kentuckians: "For my own part, I think him a great man, and I know he is an agreeable one. . . . You must have remarked one thing in him, the unequaled quickness of his mind. The rapidity with which he thinks exceeds everything I have ever witnessed in any other individual. When a new subject is presented to him he sees in an instant all its various bearings, as far at least as he will ever see them."

Clay had the power of captivating his followers and most of the people who came in contact with him. If he was at times imperious, dictatorial, and petulant, he was able to soothe an aggrieved person by his amiability. Philip Hone, the New York businessman and diarist, has described the alternation of Clay's moods and his power to hold friends despite his temperamental behavior. The Kentuckian, Hone recorded in his diary, was "quick as the lightning's flash at the slightest imputation upon his character, but mild and soothing as the summer morning when convinced (as he easily is) that himself has been to blame." At the whist table he was often "fretful, irascible and arbitary; but there is a sort of devotional feeling on the part of his familiar friends which make them submit to behavior which would not be tolerated in another. He is in fact the spoiled child of society; everybody loves him, subscribes to his opinions, and finds excuses for his foibles."

Clay was fond of pleasantry and persiflage, and had a natural and unpretentious manner and an easy, nonchalant air. He was never awed by the presence of anyone, and in any group his confidence was so assured that he naturally took the lead. He was unlearned in metaphysics, rhetoric, or logic, but this deficiency did not bother him in the least, for "he had a hearty contempt for all three of them." A very pronounced characteristic of Clay was his never-failing optimism and buoyancy of temperament. Yet he suffered from a delicately strung nervous system which made him so responsive to emotion and gave his face and voice such great expressiveness. "He was the most emotional man I ever knew," J. O. Harrison, his close associate and executor, commented.

From other descriptions of Clay and from his correspondence there emerges the portrait of an early Victorian gentleman. Sentimental, tears easily gushing, courteous in a formal way, he exhibited the Victorian's sense of decorum and dignity. Unlike Webster, who had almost an indecent craving for money, Clay valued honor and the respect of people above the possession of wealth. He loved the adulation of the crowd and yet he would not succumb to low arts or to corruption to gain it. Indeed, his sense of honor was at times quixotic. Despite his gallantry to women, which was a fashion of his age, he was a faithful and considerate husband, if being absent from home for long periods while he was in Congress be not held against him. His faults were chiefly those which arose out of a high spirit and an unquenchable ambition for public office. There was nothing petty or mean about Henry Clay. Few people who knew him personally, whether they were Whigs or Democrats, could resist the charm of his warm and impulsive nature.

X I

The Great Defeat

In 1844 Clay was sixty-seven years old, at a period when most men are content to retire. Yet in this year he reached the climactic moment of his life. The presidential election of 1844 was to be Clay's last chance for the supreme goal of his ambition. His long service in public office, his ability, and his experience entitled him to expect this high office. He would have made a good President. If his career as Whig leader and his various statements can be accepted as a chart of the course he would have pursued if elected President in 1844, there would have been no war with Mexico. Expansionist though he was — and no statesman had a greater conception of the westward advance of the American people — he did not believe in war as the instrument for effecting the dream of manifest destiny.

Clay's frustrations have a pathetic quality. He was much abler than Van Buren, Harrison, Tyler, possibly Polk, and Zachary Taylor, who won the coveted prize in his era. His personality also was far more engaging than that of any of these successful candidates. He was a man of high principles who would not stoop to any dishonorable trick or deal to win office. Perhaps the most quoted of Clay's remarks was his statement "I would rather be right than be President." To a woman correspondent who requested a lock of his hair and his autograph and asked whether he had made the famous remark, he replied, "I expressed that sentiment to which you refer that I would rather be right than be President; but it has been applauded beyond its merit." Clay's defeats may show that the ill-educated democracy of his period preferred mediocre to brilliant, high-minded men as leaders. But there was another deeper reason why Clay never realized his great ambition.

While he was in retirement at Ashland his friends, abetted by the old statesman, laid plans to win him the Whig nomination in 1844. The young Whigs of New York City arranged for Epes Sargent, a Northern man, to prepare a eulogistic biography in 1842, and the next year Horace Greeley published a volume of his speeches. Clay wrote to Whig leaders advising measures to discredit and isolate Tyler still further. Clay clubs were organized, particularly in the Northeast. Webster returned to the Whig party and gave his support to the Clay candidacy, although Clay refused to enter into any bargain with the adherents of the Massachusetts statesman such as supporting him for the vice-presidential nomination.

Among his most effective campaign maneuvers were his trips into the Southern states. Here he was weakest. Although he had journeyed to New England three times he had never been in the South Atlantic states. He had a good excuse to go to New Orleans for his health, stopping at Natchez and Baton Rouge to make speeches before enthusiastic crowds. Clay's tariff policies were favorable to the Louisiana sugar planters and he was warmly supported by them. After spending two months of the winter of 1843-1844 in New Orleans, he set out in the spring for this unvisited region on his way to Washington. He tried to avoid giving his tour the appearance of electioneering for office. He requested his friends along his route to protect him from crowds, for his health would not stand speaking at too many places. Nevertheless, he had a triumphal progress from New Orleans to Mobile, through Macon, Savannah, Augusta, Raleigh, Petersburg, and Norfolk to Washington.

Clay had already decided upon a safe and conservative platform. He had concluded to follow political expediency and not press for the restoration of the old Bank of the United States. Instead, he advocated an amendment of the Constitution to limit the President to a single term of office, restrictions on the exercise of the veto power, the distribution of the proceeds of the sale of public lands among the states, a tariff law that would give equitable protection to American industry, and a sound national currency. Particularly did he try to make his tariff views palatable to the Southern people by arguing that a protective tariff which permitted fair competition between domestic and foreign manufacturers would result in lower prices for manufactured goods to the American consumers.

Clay did not foresee that the real issue of the campaign was to be not any of the issues which he desired to bring forward, but the annexation of Texas. He and the Whig politicians tried desperately to suppress this issue during the campaign, for it was so closely tied with the expansion of slavery that the Whig candidate could not take a firm position on it without alienating a large body of his followers either in the North or the South. Furthermore, he was embarrassed by the fact that his state was strongly in favor of the annexation of Texas. Kentucky had many close ties with the Lone Star Republic. A native son, Albert Sidney Johnston, was Secretary of War of the Southern republic; many Kentuckians had relatives living there, and Clay's most influential supporters, General Leslie Combs and John J. Crittenden, each had a son who had recently participated in Texan military expeditions. When Combs's seventeen-year-old son was captured in the Santa Fé expedition, the "Kentucky Rifle" went to Texas and wrote a strong letter urging the annexation of that country.

Clay argued publicly and in letters to politicians that the presidential campaign of 1844 was not a suitable occasion in which to present the disturbing and highly divisive question of Texas annexation to the voters. Anticipating that Martin Van Buren would be the Democratic nominee for President, he invited him to visit Kentucky. Van Buren accepted and in May, 1842, the inscrutable Democratic politician came to Ashland to talk to the Whig leader. No one knows whether they made any commitments, explicit or implicit, to each other, but it seems probable that they agreed to eliminate the Texas annexation issue from the campaign.

By the spring of 1844 popular sentiment in the South and West in favor of annexation of Texas, however, had become so great that Clay felt forced to make a public statement of his position. Tyler had already made an explosive issue of the subject by negotiating a treaty with Texas for annexation which was signed on April 12, 1844, the day Clay arrived in Raleigh. Calhoun, the Secretary of State, had stirred up the antislavery people of the North by a letter to the English minister, Lord Aberdeen, in which he declared that the annexation of Texas was necessary for the preservation of Southern slavery.

The Texas issue placed Clay in a serious dilemma which he tried to resolve by the Raleigh letter of April 17, 1844. His correspondence at this period indicates that he did a lot of wishful thinking; for example, he commented that he had found during his progress from New Orleans to Raleigh "a degree of indifference or opposition to annexation that surprised me." Nevertheless, he decided at Raleigh that it was expedient to write a letter to the public explaining his views in regard to the annexation of Texas. This he sent to Senator Crittenden in Washington for publication, informing him that the Whig leaders of North Carolina concurred in believing that it was his duty to publish his sentiments on Texas. Because he suspected that Crittenden doubted the wisdom of such a publication, when he arrived at Petersburg he dispatched another letter to the Senator declaring that he was perfectly confident of the good effect that his Raleigh letter would have and therefore he could not consent to its suppression or to unnecessary delay in its publication.

The Raleigh letter has generally been regarded as a political straddle, designed to conciliate both the Northern antislavery men and the Southern annexationists. In it Clay pointed out that the immediate annexation of Texas would lead to a war with Mexico, would threaten the integrity of the union, and would saddle a great debt upon the country. Furthermore, it was not desired or called for, he wrote, by a large portion of the people of the United States. He declared that the annexation of Texas was not a proper question to be decided in a presidential campaign. The voters had enough pressing subjects of internal policy to consider. He was opposed therefore, he said, to the annexation of the Lone Star Republic "at this time." The letter was published in the great Whig organ, the *National Intelligencer,* on April 27, the same day on which Van Buren issued a letter in the *Washington Globe* taking almost the same position.

The Raleigh letter had no serious effect on Clay's standing with the Whigs. On May 1 their convention at Baltimore unanimously nominated him and then chose Theodore Frelinghuysen of New Jersey as their candidate for Vice President. The Democratic convention at the end of May disappointed Clay by nominating the dark-horse candidate James Knox Polk of Tennessee. Their platform called for "the re-occupation of Oregon and the re-annexation of Texas at the earliest practicable period."

The Texas issue was not scotched but animated by the defeat of the Calhoun treaty of annexation in the Senate on June 8. All the Whig senators except one voted against it. The Southern Whigs were on the defensive, nevertheless, in regard to the Texas issue, and they tried to conciliate opinion in their section by saying that their candidate was in favor of the acquisition of Texas but "not just yet." In order to soothe public opinion in the South, Clay wrote his first Alabama letter on July 1. He declared that he personally had no objection to the annexation of Texas but that he was unwilling to see it made an issue which "jeoparded" [sic] the Union. He protested against the position of the extremists of South Carolina who wished to make the recent rejection of the Texas treaty an occasion to dissolve the Union. In a noble passage he declared, "If anyone desire to know the leading and paramount object of my public life, the preservation of this Union will furnish the key."

But Clay continued to be disturbed by fears that his position on Texas would be interpreted against him in the slave states; on July 27 he wrote a second Alabama letter. In this unlucky pronouncement he said that he would be glad to see Texas added to the Union if it could be accomplished "without national dishonor, without war, with the general consent of the States of the Union, and upon fair and reasonable terms." The question of annexation he thought should not be decided with reference to slavery, which was a transient institution, but on the basis of its value to the country, for Texas would be "a permanent acquisition which would last as long as the globe remains."

The Alabama letters were fatal to Clay's prospects of winning the Presidency. Not only did they alienate many antislavery people in that region, but Clay's repudiation of

Cassius Marcellus Clay, the Kentucky antislavery crusader, strengthened the hostility of the abolitionists. Cassius Marcellus had offered his services to his distinguished cousin, and when Clay accepted, began a strenuous tour of speech-making in the free states, depicting Henry Clay as an emancipationist. When accounts of the speeches of the zealous antislavery reformer began to circulate in the slave states, Clay was alarmed and wrote to him to exercise circumspection in his public remarks. The latter offered to abandon the campaign, but Clay told him to continue prudently. He regretted the necessity of repudiating his cousin, but his advisers had warned him that he would otherwise lose some of the slave states and might not even carry Kentucky.

The campaign developed great enthusiasm, excitement, and bitter recrimination. Clay was confident that his party would win a more glorious victory than it had in 1840. The Whigs were stirred to great efforts at barbecues and conventions at which eloquent orators such as the famed Seargent S. Prentiss spoke. John S. Littell published a short life of Clay and a collection of Whig songs entitled *The Clay Minstrel, or National Songster*. One of the songs, set to the tune "Away up Salt River," was called "Now Let Us Try Harry!":

> Near four years ago the country was stirred
> By the Whigs who resolved that they would be heard.
> They elected their President, Tippecanoe,
> They elected another, a Traitor to you.

> *Chorus*

> Now let us try Harry, now let us try Harry!
> Now let us try Harry, who always was true!

Ladies of Whig families became ardent partisans of "Gallant Harry of the West." At Clay balls, providing funds for the campaign, they danced the relatively new steps of the waltz and the gallopade, which were viewed with stern disapproval by religious leaders and members of the old generation as lascivious embraces and worldly amusement. Philip Hone commented in his diary that Harrison had been sung into the Presidency, and now Clay might be danced into the White House.

Clay's long career in politics made him vulnerable to slander and innuendo. In the spring of 1843 James Knox Polk brought up the old bargain-and-corruption story. Clay challenged him to a public debate in Tennessee and proposed that a jury of twelve Whigs and twelve Democrats decide whether Polk had slandered him. Democratic partisans contrasted the alleged immoral life of Clay with the stern purity of their standard-bearer. Polk had not gambled, while Clay's gaming was notorious. Polk was not a drunkard like the Kentucky Senator; nor had he fought duels or contributed to the death of a congressman in a duel; nor was he a man of loose morals, a horse racer, and an addict to profanity.

Clay felt the stings of these libels to such an extent that he had articles published in the newspapers to defend himself. He gathered testimony to show that he had tried to discourage the duel in which Representative William Graves of Kentucky had killed Representative Jonathan Cilley of Maine in 1838. He had even urged that the police be called to stop it. Moreover, the Whigs retorted to the slanders of their candidate by accusing Polk of having a Tory grandfather, by propagating the story that Polk branded his slaves, and by asking the sarcastic question, "Who is James K. Polk?"

James K. Polk won by an electoral vote of 170 to 105, but his popular majority was only 38,000. Clay lost the South, with the exception of Kentucky and Tennessee. But his irreparable loss was in the states of Pennsylvania and New York. In Pennsylvania Polk's actual opposition to a protective tariff was misrepresented by the Democratic

claim that he stood for "reasonable incidental protection."
In New York the Democrats put up a strong candidate for
governor, Silas Wright, who boosted the strength of the national ticket. Furthermore, the balance of power was held
by the abolitionists, who voted for James G. Birney, the
Liberty party candidate. Polk won New York by only 5016
votes, while Birney polled 15,182. It is probable that Birney drew enough antislavery Whigs away from Clay to defeat "Harry of the West."

The result of the voting came as a wholly unexpected
shock to Clay and to his friends. They sought to account
for it by various hypotheses. Clay believed that gross frauds
had been practiced against the Whigs, especially in natu-
ralizing foreigners in New York, the pivotal state. Also he
thought that the abolition vote and the foreign Catholic
vote, sensitive to the native American movement, had
weakened the Whigs in the North. Actually, Clay's defeat
was largely due to his own blunders, and particularly to
his misconception of political realities that led him to
write his letters on the Texas question. His shrewd friends
had feared that he would not keep silent but would injure
himself by freely talking and writing on political subjects;
and he had realized their fears. Furthermore, he failed to
gauge the democratic sentiment of the people; his program
had little appeal to the poor man and to the land-hungry
Westerners. When he was defeated, it was not the little
people who wept, but those who wore broadcloth suits and
tall hats and had money invested in stocks and large plantations.

After the great defeat the "Sage of Ashland" was deluged
with letters of condolence. Unnerved, he dreaded to open
his mail. One of these letters, from Philip Hone, the New
York merchant, contained an unconsciously ironical comment on the election when he observed that nine tenths of
"our respectable citizens," the merchants, the professional

men, the mechanics and workingmen, those who went to church on Sunday, voted for Clay. A correspondent from Pittsburg wrote, "You had nine-tenths of the virtue, intelligence, and respectability of the nation on our side." The blow affected Clay so deeply that he considered his public life at an end; and when the Kentucky presidential electors, after casting their votes for him at Frankfort, came as a body to pay respect to him at Ashland his address seemed a valedictory.

"Prince Hal's" youthful spirit and resiliency kept him in politics. In the spring of 1846, at the age of sixty-nine, he still hoped to be elected President. William H. Seward, then visiting Clay at Ashland, found the old statesman in vigorous health and joyous spirits, "as confident of the nomination and of success next time as he was at the last." To Daniel Mallory, Clay wrote on October 12, 1846, "I have never said that I would or would not be a candidate at the next election. I have remained perfectly passive." He was pleased by the celebration of his birthday anniversary by the young Whigs of New York City on April 12, 1847. A menu of this occasion, preserved in the Huntington Library, lists a fabulous variety of food. The game, for example, included venison with wine sauce, wild goose, snipe, squab, plover, blue-winged teal, canvasback duck, quail, rabbit, and prairie hen.

One of his enthusiastic supporters in New York was Daniel Ullmann, and to him Clay wrote in May, 1847, strongly opposing the nomination of General Zachary Taylor by the Whigs. He declared himself opposed to the nomination of a military man for President. The selection of Taylor, who was absolutely without experience in civil administration, would set a precedent that would lead to the elevation of a succession of military chiefs. He suggested that if General Scott were successful in Mexico, a collision of the political ambitions of the two generals might make it expedient to put aside both of them and to select a civilian. As to himself, he proposed to remain passive. He would consent to run if a great popular demonstration in his favor was made. Up until the battle of Buena Vista, he had believed that the mass of the Whig party had determined to bring him forward as their candidate in the next election.

In the summer of 1847, following the death of his son on the battlefield of Buena Vista, Henry Clay joined the Episcopal Church. This was doubtless a perfectly sincere act on his part, but it did make him a more suitable presidential candidate. In this summer, also, he seems to have been meditating on a proper platform for the Whig party. To Ullmann he declared that Taylor should be forced to abandon his nonpartisan stand and declare his political principles. As to his own opinion of a proper platform he thought it best to rely on the old issues, except the United States Bank. He recommended, first, the preservation of the principle of tariff protection; second, "the Mexican war, its causes, the manner of conducting it, and the great National debt which it fastens on the country"; and finally, the alarming increase of presidential vetoes and the growth of the executive power.

In this letter also he made his availability clear. His plan to visit Cape May for the sea baths was no sign that his health was bad; on the contrary it was very good, better than it had been during the last campaign. He defied old age. He had never before enjoyed the delights of sea bathing. Here he sported gallantly in the water, ducking lady companions and being ducked by them. Delegations of Whigs came from Northern cities, notably a delegation of one hundred and twenty-five from New York, to invite him to visit them. He was pleased at these evidences of his popularity and made graceful speeches, impeccably free of dangerous political content.

Clay strengthened his position as a presidential candidate among the Northern Whigs by a speech on the Mexican War in Lexington, Kentucky, on November 13, 1847. He traced the origin of the conflict to the annexation of Texas, but he expressed the opinion that even after this mistake had been made war might have been averted had Taylor been permitted to remain at Corpus Christi as he wished. The declaration of war, he observed, contained in its preamble a palpable falsehood, accusing Mexico of commencing hostilities. Indeed, the United States by its aggression against our weak Latin-American neighbor had lost the good opinion of the world; all nations looked upon us "in the prosecution of the present war as being actuated by a spirit of rapacity and an inordinate desire for territorial aggrandizement." He advised Congress to define the purpose and objects of the war. He was willing to accept the fact of the annexation of Texas and to seek a proper and just boundary for this acquisition. But Congress should definitely renounce any intention to annex Mexico. Most important of all, he wanted a disavowal of the desire "to acquire any foreign territory whatever, for the purpose of propagating slavery, or of introducing slaves from the United States into, such foreign territory."

This statement strongly leaned in the direction of the Wilmot Proviso, introduced the previous year, which had provided that any territory which might be acquired from Mexico should be free from slavery. Clay in a letter to Horace Greeley written shortly after his Lexington speech observed that he did not mention the Wilmot Proviso by name, for "it was not necessary to touch it and sufficient for the day is the evil thereof." He added that he would decide during the following spring whether he would become a candidate for the Whig nomination. Slyly he sought Seward's support by saying to the latter's close political associate that he was entirely friendly to Seward, who should be considered for Vice President or at least for a high office in a Whig administration. He concluded with a rather sad glance at his mistakes of 1844: "I mean if I should be a Candidate to write no letters, make no speeches, and be mute. I expect if that contingency should arise, to be much abused for my silence, as I have been for my speaking or writing."

In early April, 1848, Clay became an open candidate for the nomination. He believed that the Taylor boom was on the decline; he had been assured of the support of the crucial state, Ohio; and he did not know that some of the most powerful Whig leaders were secretly working against him, that his closest political friend, Senator John J. Crittenden, was discouraging any movement in his behalf, arguing that he could not be elected and that therefore the Whigs should take Taylor. The Southern Whigs were deluded into believing that because Taylor owned a plantation in Louisiana he would favor proslavery expansion. As rumors of such defections came to his ears Clay thought that the masses were for his nomination and that only some of the politicians were against him.

Before the Whig convention met in Philadelphia on June 7, however, Clay's candidacy had been seriously injured by the disloyalty of some of his former supporters in Kentucky, notably Crittenden. The Whig state convention failed to nominate Clay; a majority of the Kentucky delegates to the national convention were actually for Taylor. This early desertion by his native state presaged his defeat in the convention. On the first ballot Taylor received 111 votes, Clay 97, Scott 43, and Webster 22. On the fourth ballot Taylor was nominated and Millard Fillmore, a strong Clay man, was chosen as candidate for Vice President. Taylor's nomination was a victory of expediency, which was further indicated by the fact that the convention failed, as in 1840, to adopt a platform.

Clay was deeply hurt by his rejection. He felt that the Whigs had abandoned all devotion to principles and had chosen a military man solely because of his availability. He had a low opinion of Taylor, whom he believed to be wholly incompetent for the duties of the Presidency. He was particularly grieved by the conduct of the Kentucky delegation. He did not know whether he should ever again pass the mountains, and to Nicholas Dean he confessed at the same time, "I consider my public career forever terminated." He refused to run as an independent candidate; it was best quietly to submit. At the end of September he commented bitterly, "I have been so opposed to the election of a *mere* military character to the Presidency that I hold myself in reserve whether I shall vote at all."

During his long career in politics Clay had been candidate for election to the Presidency five times, but only in the election of 1844 did he come close to winning. His splendid personality, his eloquence, and his distinguished career in Congress were unavailing. Clay had made serious blunders in political strategy. But there was also an important element in the political situation of the period 1824-1848 which explained his frustration. After the defeat of 1844, Philip Hone of New York City and many another respectable Whig concluded that the country would not choose a statesman, a man of superior talent, to occupy the executive office. The "Old Prince" carried the banner of a party whose dominant element was aristocratic, the wealthy business interests of the North, the large planters, and conservative men generally. It is significant that after the election he expressed his gratitude to his friend John M. Clayton for the vote of Delaware, especially sending his thanks to the Du Ponts for their "friendly and powerful aid." Thus Clay was out of step with the march of a democracy, with the masses; for the United States of the 1830's and 1840's was a growing young country whose natural temper and interest were democratic. Furthermore, he was a moderate at a time when the nation was being polarized over the slavery question. Finally, the "Sage of Ashland" made his candidacy on a platform of issues that were largely outmoded.

But although he had been defeated in the great ambitions of his life, he still had one supreme service to render to the nation.

X I I

Portrait of a Nationalist

IN THE FALL OF 1848 Clay was practicing law with his son James and supervising the operations of the plantation at Ashland. Norwithstanding his success in the legal profession, as he had grown older he seems to have thoroughly disliked the practice of law. After his retirement from the Secretaryship of State, he declared that he did not intend to practice law, for, he asserted, "Nothing but necessity will compel me to put on the harness again." While he served in the Senate, however, he supplemented his salary by pleading before the Supreme Court. When he was nearly seventy years old, in July, 1846, he argued his last great criminal case. He defended Lafayette Shelby, a grandson of the first governor of Kentucky, who had deliberately killed a young clerk in front of Lexington's principal hotel. So large was the crowd who tried to hear the great orator speak in Fayette County Court House that the court adjourned to the more spacious Morrison Hall of Transylvania University. Here Clay spoke for two hours and fifteen minutes and, although the evidence against his client was overwhelming, succeeded in dividing the jury, with the result that no verdict was returned. Shel⊦

was released from jail on bail and thus was able to flee to Texas, never to be punished. The citizenry were so incensed at this miscarriage of justice, which they attributed to the influence of family and wealth, that they burned the judge in effigy.

Despite the demands of his law office and his farm, Clay's mind was preoccupied with political affairs. He was solicitous that his followers should not be proscribed by the President-elect in the distribution of patronage. But Taylor was jealous of Clay and showed little magnanimity. Clay wrote to his friend Leslie Combs that he desired a good federal appointment for him, but he said, "I have no proof of any desire [of the President] to confer or consult with me on any subject." Although Taylor granted his request for an appointment for his son James by giving to him a diplomatic post in Portugal, he wounded the pride of the old statesman by letting it be known that Clay had applied for the office.

The "Sage of Ashland," as he was now called, visited New Orleans for his health in the winter of 1848-1849. Here he suffered a serious fall down a stairway at the home of his friend Dr. Mercer which incapacitated him for five or six weeks. Before he left Lexington he had told his friends that he would not become a formal or avowed candidate for the Senate, but if the General Assembly should wish to elect him he would accept the office out of "a sense of public duty and the hope of doing some good." His wish was gratified, for in January, 1849, the legislators elected him. His friends and probably Clay himself wished thereby to prove that despite his recent rejection by the Kentucky Whig delegation as its candidate for President, the "Sage of Ashland" was still a great political power in the state. The supporters of Taylor feared that the election of the old Whig warhorse would make trouble for the new administration; but Clay had already decided on a policy of cooperation, provided the President pursued Whig principles.

When he arrived at Washington he took lodgings at the National Hotel, paying $30 a week for a bedroom and a parlor. He was very comfortable and enjoyed the services of an excellent valet, a free Negro. Although his health was bad he walked from the hotel to the sessions of Congress on Capitol Hill. Here through the hot summer he was conscientious in daily occupying his seat in the Senate. He was not an intent listener, however, for spectators in the gallery could observe him taking snuff and eating striped peppermint candy.

Clay realized that the great struggle in Congress over the organization of the Western territories would severely try the strength of the Union. Southerners were incensed over the demand for the passage of the Wilmot Proviso, excluding slavery from the territory acquired from Mexico. On November 13 California adopted an antislavery constitution and applied for admission to the Union. Mississippi, instigated by a letter from Calhoun, summoned a Southern convention to meet in Nashville in June, 1850, to concert measures to resist Northern "aggressions." Shortly after Congress met, Calhoun called a meeting of the members from the slave states for the purpose of a Union of the South to protect Southern rights. Many of the Southern Whigs opposed this movement, but those who did attend Calhoun's meeting issued an address of the "Southern Delegates in Congress to their Constituents" which was a document ominous to the preservation of the Union.

Clay sought to persuade Kentucky to take a strong public stand against the growing disunion sentiment in the South. In December he wrote to Leslie Combs, the powerful Whig leader in the Bluegrass region, urging him to promote public meetings to pass resolutions of strong devotion to the Union. Clay had found that the feeling among intemperate Southern politicians was stronger in favor of disunion than he had thought possible, but he believed that the sentiment of the masses, generally, in the South was sound. He sent to Combs some suitable resolutions to be adopted by the Kentuckians. Clay's plan of manipulating public opinion in the state in favor of a strong condemnation of disunion was carried out.

In December President Taylor sent a message to Congress recommending the admission of California into the Union with its free-state constitution. The Southerners arose in arms against the admission of the state without adequate compensation to Southern interests. Taylor, who had fallen under the influence of the antislavery Senator William H. Seward of New York, however, was adamant in insisting that California be admitted without reference to other considerations. Some compromise was essential, for the entrance of the territory as a free state would upset the previous equilibrium of free- and slave-state representatives in the Senate.

The situation was tense. Clay observed that there was a considerable majority in the House of Representatives, and probably one in the Senate, in favor of passing the Wilmot Proviso. The Hotspurs of the South were proclaiming their determination to bring about a dissolution of the Union if this should happen. He was thinking of bringing forward a "comprehensive scheme of settling amicably the whole question in all its bearings."

Clay was the logical and the most influential man in Congress to initiate such an adjustment. On January 29 he introduced in the Senate his plan of compromise in the form of eight resolutions. His proposals contained little originality, for most of them had been previously suggested. Clay recommended that Congress pass bills admitting California into the Union with its antislavery constitution, organizing the remainder of the territory acquired from Mexico into two huge territories "without the adoption of any restriction or condition on the subject of slavery," paying a part of the national debt of Texas in return for the abandonment of the Texan claim to a large area east of the Rio Grande, which was to be included in the New Mexico territory, abolishing the slave trade in the District of Columbia, enacting a more effective fugitive-slave law, and passing a resolution denying the power of Congress to prohibit or obstruct the interstate slave trade.

Clay's resolutions provoked an immediate dissent from Senator Jefferson Davis of Mississippi, who took strong exception to the statement in Clay's second resolution that "slavery does not exist by law, and is not likely to be introduced into any of the territory acquired by the United States from the Republic of Mexico." Davis asserted that the compromise offered nothing valuable to the South. The minimum concession which the South could afford to accept was for Congress to extend the Missouri Compromise line to the Pacific and give legal sanction to slavery south of that line. Clay rose to say that no earthly power could force him to vote to establish slavery where it did not exist. Americans blamed England, he exclaimed, for forcing African slavery upon the colonies, and he would not have the posterity of California and New Mexico reproach him for voting to impose the institution upon a free territory.

On February 5 and 6 Clay made one of the most significant speeches of his life. As he walked up the long flight of stairs leading to the Capitol, he stopped several times to recover his breath and he seemed very feeble. But when his companions suggested that he defer his speech he refused. His country was in danger. The Senate Chamber was crowded with people, among them many ladies in crinoline, expecting to hear a great oratorical tour de force. Clay warned his audience, however, that the occasion was too serious for oratorical display or for "any extraordinary ornament or decoration of speech." His remarks were primarily an appeal to reason, employing facts and solid arguments, as well as an appeal to the patriotic feelings of Americans.

Clay sought to get both sides of the controversy to make concessions. He attributed the perilous state of the nation to the prevalence of violent party spirit. Believing that slavery did not exist in the Western Territory when it was acquired, for Mexican law prohibited it, he expressed the opinion that slavery never would be introduced there. "You have got what is worth a thousand Wilmot Provisos," he said. "You have got nature itself on your side." California had a right to establish a free constitution and the South should not oppose this exercise of democracy. He condemned the slave trade in the District of Columbia with its spectacle of corteges of manacled slaves passing through the streets of Washington, but he also declared that it was a duty of the Northern states to return fugitive slaves, especially family slaves, who, he said, "are treated with the kindness that the children of the family receive." He urged Southern congressmen to remember that all the territory which the United States had acquired prior to the Mexican War had been opened to slavery and therefore they should be willing to make concessions now in regard to the new territory by not seeking to force their peculiar institutions into this region. He warned them that secession was not a legal right and would be followed by a disastrous civil war. Clay's great speech was greeted with enthusiasm and many of his admirers, male and female, rushed up to congratulate him and to kiss him.

If comparison is the key to understanding, the debate over the compromise of 1850 affords an excellent opportunity to measure Clay against other statesmen of his time. The outstanding participants in the debate were spokesmen for the sections into which the United States was divided. Calhoun's famous fourth of March speech, representing the viewpoint of the cotton South, contained elements of fanaticism. He was obsessed with the idea that the South was growing weaker as the years rolled by and that it should force the issue now. He demanded the impossible, that the Northern states should suppress the agitation of the abolitionists, open the territories to slavery, and restore the political equilibrium between the free and the slave states. His speech, with its Roman overtones, was far more succinct than Clay's, more logical, and, to use a favorite word of the 1840's, more "chaste" in style. But it lacked understanding of the American nation, of the irreversible processes of time and growth, of the need of reasonable compromise which characterized Clay's long, discursive oration.

Two prominent Northern spokesmen of public opinion, Webster and William H. Seward of New York, represented conflicting points of view in their section. Webster's seventh of March speech was dominated by a spirit of patriotism and moderation similar to that of Clay, the conservative Whig spirit, but he expressed his thoughts in a more philosophical and literary form. No phrase in the Kentuckian's speech lives in the memory like the statement of the Massachusetts orator, "I would not take pains uselessly to reaffirm an ordinance of nature nor to re-enact the will of God."

William H. Seward on March 11 represented the sentiment of the Northern extremists when he declared that compromise was essentially vicious, involving a surrender of principle, and when he demanded that the territories be closed to slavery. His assertion, "But there is a higher law than the Constitution," was shocking to conservatives like Clay and to Southerners in general. Antislavery men in the North, on the other hand, viewed it as inspired by a moral idealism lacking in the speeches of the compromisers. But in reality Seward was a practical politician who often spoke for political effect and expediency, whereas Clay was undoubtedly sincere and disinterested in his efforts to compose differences between the North and the South.

The method of voting on the compromise proposals proved to be of vital importance. The Southerners were afraid that if the California bill should be adopted first the North would refuse to pass other bills compensating the South for its concession. They therefore wished the various measures of compromise combined in one omnibus bill. Clay at first was opposed to this method but finally concluded that it offered the best chance for the success of compromise. Accordingly, he supported the resolution of Senator Henry S. Foote of Mississippi that a grand committee be appointed for this purpose to which his own proposals as well as the plan of John Bell of Tennessee should be submitted. The Senate adopted the resolution on April 17 and a Committee of Thirteen with Clay as chairman was elected by ballot.

On May 8 Clay presented the comprehensive report of the committee. It recommended essentially the same measures as his original compromise proposals, except that his resolution that Congress had no power to prohibit or obstruct the interstate slave trade was dropped. In the debate that followed during the hot Washington summer, Clay was faithful in his attendance and led the debate for the adoption of the Omnibus bill. But he had the weight of the executive against him as well as the opposition of both the Southern and Northern ultras. The death of President Taylor on July 9, following a sickness caused by partaking bountifully of cherries and iced milk on a blistering hot day, removed a roadblock that frustrated the compromisers. Millard Fillmore, who succeeded as President, was a friend of Clay's and facilitated the passage of Compromise measures. The Texas bondholders were also at work.

Even with this help the compromisers found that they could not obtain a majority in the Senate for the Omnibus bill. On July 31 came a crucial vote on Clay's compromise in which a majority of the Whigs deserted Clay and contributed heavily to defeat the Omnibus bill. Finally Stephen A. Douglas led a movement to separate the components of the Omnibus bill into separate measures. This method proved the strategy of victory and it was adopted after Clay had retired from Congress to Newport for rest and recuperation in August. Under the leadership of Douglas the various bills that ultimately composed the Compromise of 1850, with the exception of the District of Columbia bill, were passed. When Clay returned he took charge of the last-named bill, which was passed by Congress on September 17. The compromise had been effected by the use of a cab instead of an omnibus. More Democratic than Whig votes contributed to the victory.

On October 2 Clay returned to Lexington from his great triumph in Washington. The citizens welcomed him with the firing of cannon, the ascent of rockets, the blaze of bonfires, and the ringing of the church bells. As he descended from his high coach in front of the Phoenix Hotel a huge crowd gave three long cheers. Clay proceeded into the hotel and addressed the crowd from the balcony. His voice was clear, full, sonorous, like the ringing of a bell, and so distinct that every syllable could be heard. He congratulated his audience on the fact that the recent compromise had saved the Union. With a charming appeal to the sensibilities of his audience, he concluded, pointing his finger in the direction of Ashland, while the crowd set up a laugh and cheers, "There lives an old lady about a mile and a half from here, with whom I have lived for more than fifty years, whom I would rather see than any of you," and bowing gracefully he withdrew while the crowd sent up many a merry peal of laughter, mingled with hearty cheers.

Clay returned to Congress in the fall of 1850, but the brief remainder of his career there was an anticlimax. His health was bad as the result of a severe cold and a debilitating cough. Nevertheless, he attended a concert of Jenny Lind, where the audience rose and gave him an ovation which greatly pleased him. His chief contributions in this last year of his life were his strong support of the compromise, including the Fugitive Slave Act, which was under attack in the North, and his opposition to intervening in the internal affairs of Austria to aid the independence of Hungary. Kossuth, the Hungarian revolutionist, had made a special visit to Clay at the National Hotel to secure his aid, but the "Sage of Ashland," grown conservative and cautious, resisted his appeal. In the spring of 1851 he returned to Kentucky by way of a sea voyage to Cuba in an effort to benefit his health.

In December the frail old statesman returned to Congress, but his health declined so seriously that he could not make any more speeches. On December 17, 1851, he announced that he would resign his seat the next year. But before he could do so, he died in the National Hotel in Washington on June 29, 1852. He died with calmness and fortitude after months of wasting illness. His body was transported with much pomp and ceremony home to Ashland, from where he was buried in the Lexington Cemetery in the presence of the nation's dignitaries. There an imposing column now marks his grave.

At the very end of his life the Whigs of New York presented to the old statesman a medal made of pure California gold, inscribed with a record of his achievements. It listed the following events: "Senate, 1806; Speaker, 1811; War of 1812 with Great Britain; Ghent, 1814; Spanish

America, [1818 to] 1822; Missouri Compromise, 1821; American System, 1824; Greece, 1824; Secretary of State, 1825; Panama Instructions, 1826; Tariff Compromise, 1833; Public Domain, 1833-1841; Peace with France Preserved, 1835; Compromise, 1850." Clay himself had suggested the citations. He referred to his work in securing appropriations over a series of years for the Cumberland or National Road. He also took particular pride in his Panama Instructions, with its exposition of liberal principles in regard to maritime war and neutral rights, which he adjudged to be the ablest state paper that he composed as Secretary of State. He likewise regarded highly his report to the Senate on the proper course in regard to the French spoliation claims. He believed that his report preserved the peace "against the whole weight of Jackson."

Clay's policy in foreign affairs had strengthened the prestige of the nation. He had won the friendship of the South American countries struggling to free themselves from Spain's grip. Harriet Martineau observed that Clay's speeches were read at the head of the armies of the South American republics. At an early date he had presented a broad vision of the community of nations of the Western Hemisphere, declaring, "We are the natural head of the American family." Yet he had not favored entangling alliances with the nations of the Western world nor with those of the Old World. He envisaged a unity through moral influence and good fellowship. He was, indeed, one of the early architects of the Pan-American Union.

Clay was very proud of his "American System," and certainly he must be classed with Alexander Hamilton as one of the apostles of economic nationalism, which is still a powerful force in American policy. He was not an extremist, however, in the application of his ideas of a protective tariff and of building a "home market." "Long John" Wentworth, who lived in the same hotel as Clay in 1850, was impressed with Clay's devotion to the tariff. The old statesman received some champagne produced near Cincinnati, which he was fond of dispensing to callers in his apartment. He used this native wine as a text for the advocacy of a protective tariff. Sipping a glass of it, he would declare the country ought, if possible, to produce all that it consumed. Clay's economic nationalism anticipated the rise of the postwar industrial revolution that transformed rural America.

Clay cannot be neatly typed as a conservative or a liberal, for his career exhibited characteristics of both schools of thought. His efforts to advance the cause of gradual emancipation of the slaves in the United States belong to the category of cautious liberalism. There is evidence that Lincoln's views on slavery and colonization were strongly influenced by the views of the "Sage of Ashland." The closing lines of one of the Great Emancipator's speeches on slavery were modeled after the peroration of Clay's speech of 1827 before the American Colonization Society. Clay was also liberal in his Indian policy, in his advocacy of the recognition of the South American republics, and in his reliance upon using public opinion as a lever to move Congress. But he was conservative in many aspects of his thinking, such as his condemnation of the Dorr rebellion in Rhode Island, his land policy, his support of the business interests, his opposition to the agitation of slavery, his devotion to the Union, and his Madisonian philosophy of government.

The strength and stability of the government of the United States has developed in large measure because of a workable two-party system. Henry Clay deserves much credit for his contribution to the growth of such an arrangement in this country. A strong opposition party is vital to the sound functioning of a democracy. In the Whig party Clay developed almost a model opposition based on enlightened conservatism. He gave it vigorous leadership and dominated its councils.

Clay's most enduring claim to fame was his share in preserving the integrity of the nation during periods of violent stress. In 1820-1821 during the crisis over the admission of Missouri as a state, in 1833 during the nullification crisis, and in the Compromise of 1850 he rendered inestimable service and earned the title "The Great Pacificator" which was given to him. When the federal Union was seriously threatened in 1849-1850 he sought to revive the cult of President Washington, who symbolized to Americans the idea of nationality and patriotism. Deeply alarmed by the progress of disunion sentiment in South Carolina in 1850, he declared that no state had a right to secede and that the Union must be preserved, if necessary, by force. Ever youthful in spirit, he retained to the end of his life much of the national sentiment of the era of Washington and Madison.

Clay's great gift, the ability to reconcile conflicting groups and interests, served his country well. He had a clear realization that the only practicable way of preserving the Union was by the art of compromise, by the same method that the federal Constitution had been effected and in the same spirit in which successful marriages are continued. Clay's role was that of moderator. He believed in the principle of gradualism in politics, taking account of local conditions, emotional involvements, and long-established popular attitudes. He had faith that the ultimate improvement of society would come not by heated emotion nor by violent surgery but through reasonableness and compromise. His position as Kentucky's delegate in the Senate undoubtedly had great influence in turning him toward the use of compromise, for the people of his state were moderate in their attitude toward slavery, and their dependence on the Mississippi River with its outlet

at New Orleans was a strong nationalizing influence on
state policy. It was fortunate for the country that a man of
Clay's stature and skill in the art of politics was in Congress during the critical years of 1849 and 1850. Aided by
other leaders, notably Stephen Douglas, he was able to
persuade selfish politicians and strong sectionalists to accept the Great Compromise, which saved the unity of the
nation for ten years; and when the spirit of compromise
failed in 1860 the United States had attained the strength
to preserve its unity permanently.

The final achievement of Clay's life should have been
glory enough for any man. Yet there is a sadness in reviewing his life, for he did not attain his great personal ambition. He started his career in national politics with the
highest hopes — he was "Harry of the West," who seemed
destined to become the first President from the West. It
was a fluid period in American politics — one which permitted an exceptionally powerful personality like Clay to
achieve a leadership independent of party organization.
At this time he faithfully represented a region — the West
— which was nationalistic in outlook. By 1830, however,
the ambitious Kentuckian no longer advocated some of its
most vital interests. Andrew Jackson and Thomas Hart
Benton became pre-eminently the leaders of the growing
West. Clay drew closer to the capitalists of the Northeast.
This was a tragic change, especially for a man with a
strong Jeffersonian background. It fundamentally ex-
plains the frustrations of his personal ambition. In the latter part of his life the two-party system emerged. Within
that system there was not so much room for the powerful individual who could manage and dominate factions. In this
period Clay failed either to enact his legislative program or
to be elected President. But more important than reaching
the Presidency, to which so many mediocre men have been
elected, the greater glory was his — to save the Union.

A Note on the Sources

THE PRINCIPAL SOURCE for this study has been the xtensive collection of the papers of Henry Clay which the University of Kentucky has been assembling by means of microfilm, photostat, and typed copies of the originals, preparatory to their publication in a definitive edition. The director of this project, Professor James B. Hopkins, of the History Department of the University of Kentucky, and his associate, Dr. Mary W. Hargreaves, have given me access to this collection and have carefully read my manuscript. It would have been impossible for me to have written this biography at any other place than Lexington with such a command of the sources that are now available there. Twenty years ago Bernard Mayo wrote his excellent and colorful biography *Henry Clay, Spokesman of the New West* (Boston, 1937) and Glyndon G. Van Deusen published his scholarly and comprehensive *The Life of Henry Clay* (Boston, 1937), both based on a study of the sources available at that time. In addition to the manuscript sources which they used, the editors of the Clay papers have been able to gather much material from small and scattered collections held by private individuals, historical societies, commercial dealers, colleges and universities, and the Library of Congress.

The researcher into Clay's career living in Lexington also has the advantage of being able to visit at recurring intervals

Clay's home, Ashland, which shelters many relics of the "Sage of Ashland," and to walk in his garden and beneath the great trees, still standing, which shade its lawn. The brick house on Mill Street in which he was married to Lucretia Hart has recently been torn down to make way for a parking lot, but several of the fine old homes of Lexington, Morrison Hall of Transylvania University, and some of the Bluegrass farms still have very much the same appearance that they had over a hundred years ago when Clay used to walk down the streets of Lexington to his law office or ride out to neighboring farms to talk with their owners about hemp, corn, livestock, and politics.

The first biography of Clay was written by a brilliant Connecticut journalist, George D. Prentice, who came to Kentucky to gather material for a campaign biography, entitled *Biography of Henry Clay* (New York, 1831), and stayed to found the great Whig newspaper the *Louisville Journal*. Epes Sargent, a Northerner, also wrote a campaign biography of the Whig leader, *The Life and Public Service of Henry Clay* (New York, 1844, 2 vols.), published by the press of Horace Greeley, and Daniel Mallory published *The Life and Speeches of the Hon. Henry Clay* (New York, 1843 and 1844, 2 vols.).

The most important editor of Clay's works and also a contemporary biographer was Calvin Colton, who in the 1850's became professor of public economy at Trinity College, Hartford, Connecticut. After Clay's defeat in the election of 1844 Colton came to Lexington and remained two months talking with the great statesman and preparing a biography of him. Clay read part of his manuscript and gave his blessing to the project, which Colton published in 1846 under the title *The Life and Times of Henry Clay* (New York, 2 vols.). In 1855 he published the valuable *The Private Correspondence of Henry Clay* (New York). In the same year he published *The Works of Henry Clay* (New York, 6 vols.) which was republished in 1897 in seven volumes with an introduction by Thomas B. Reed and a history of tariff legislation from 1812 to 1896 by William McKinley.

A fundamental source in the study of the career of Clay is the record of the debates in Congress to be found in the *Annals of Congress* and *The Congressional Globe.* Here one can analyze Clay's remarkable skill in debate, his clever repartee, his parliamentary ability, his political ideas, and the oratory for which he was famed.

Many insights into Clay's personality are furnished by travelers' accounts, notably Harriet Martineau, *Retrospect of Western Travel* (London, 1838), and by the autobiographies, correspondence, and reminiscences of his contemporaries. The papers of some of his associates and opponents present a quite different view of Clay's character and political conduct than is to be found in Clay's own correspondence. This unfavorable view is particularly reflected in John Spencer Bassett (ed.), *Correspondence of Andrew Jackson* (Washington, 1929, 6 vols.); Charles Francis Adams (ed.), *Memoirs of John Quincy Adams Comprising Portion of His Diary from 1795 to 1848* (Philadelphia, 1874); J. Franklin Jameson *et al.* (eds.), "Correspondence of John C. Calhoun," *Annual Report of the American Historical Association for the Year 1899* (Washington, 1900, II); and Henry A. Wise, *Seven Decades of the Union* (Philadelphia, 1872). A more neutral view of Clay is presented in John C. Fitzpatrick (ed.), "The Autobiography of Martin Van Buren," *Annual Report of the American Historical Association for the Year 1918* (Washington, 1920, II); Thomas Hart Benton, *Thirty Years' View, or a History of the Workings of the American Government for Thirty Years from 1820 to 1850* (New York, 1854-1856); and Fletcher Pratt (ed.), *The Private Correspondence of Daniel Webster* (Boston, 1857, 2 vols.). Sources friendly to Clay include Margaret Bayard Smith, *The First Forty Years of Washington Society* (New York, 1906); Mrs. Chapman Coleman, *The Life of John J. Crittenden with Selections from His Correspondence and Speeches* (Philadelphia, 1871); Allan Nevins (ed.), *The Diary of Philip Hone* (New York, 1927, 2 vols.); Henry T. Shanks (ed.), *The Papers of Willie P. Mangum* (Raleigh, 1950-1955, 4 vols.); Henry W. Hilliard, *Politics and Pen Pictures at Home and Abroad* (New York, 1892); Nathan Sargent, *Public Men and Events* (Philadelphia, 1875); Horace Greeley, *Recollections of a Busy Life* (New York, 1868); and R. C. McGrane (ed.), *The Correspond-*

ence of Nicholas Biddle Dealing with National Affairs, 1807-1844 (Boston, 1919).

Until the publication of the biographies by Mayo and Van Deusen the outstanding biography of Clay was Carl Schurz, *Henry Clay* (Boston, 1887, 2 vols.), which was marred by Schurz's strong antislavery and nationalist bias. Joseph M. Rogers published *The True Henry Clay* (Philadelphia, 1904) and Thomas Hart Clay, grandson of the statesman, published *Henry Clay* (Philadelphia, 1910), which contained some family traditions. George R. Poage made a penetrating study of Clay in *Henry Clay and the Whig Party* (Chapel Hill, 1933). Claude Bowers, *The Party Battles of the Jackson Period* (Boston, 1922), presents a prejudiced view. Clay's career as Secretary of State is described in Samuel Flagg Bemis (ed.), *The American Secretaries of State* (New York, 1927-1929). I am indebted to Professor Jasper B. Shannon of the Political Science Department of the University of Kentucky for the privilege of reading his Ph.D. dissertation at the University of Wisconsin (1934), entitled "Henry Clay as a Political Leader." Also I have had the benefit of using the manuscript study of the Whig party in Kentucky by the late John A. Coffin, prepared under the direction of Professor William O. Lynch of the Department of History of Indiana University. I wish to acknowledge the aid I received in studying Clay's farming interests from the research of one of my graduate students, Richard Troutman, whose master's thesis at the University of Kentucky is entitled "Plantation Life in the Ante-Bellum Bluegrass Region of Kentucky" (1955).

Index

Henry Clay is abbreviated HC.